Praise For *2*

"This is a "must read" book tha
and advice to anyone trying to answer the universal questions of "Where do my struggles lie?" and "How can I overcome them?" I was very impressed by the courage and vulnerability expressed by these "beautiful women," who openly share their stories, their self-doubts, and ultimately their victories and wisdom. I couldn't put it down."

–Dennis Kennedy, *CEO of National Diversity Council*

"20 Beautiful Women is a daily read for continuous inspiration! There is nothing more refreshing than hearing from women who speak their own truth with power, conviction and genuine raw emotion. I found myself immersed in their journeys and their outlook on life through the experiences that were shared. This book fed my soul."

–Shelly Walker Benes, *author of H.A.I.R to be released 2015*

"I LOVE THIS BOOK! Who would have ever known, a book with various stories about women's lives could relate to a male as myself. I love how each story deals with various situations and obstacles women go through on a day-to-day base. I believe each one will not only help women overcome their fear of flaws but join hands with those who have gone through similar situations, letting them know they are not alone."

–Sebastian Mosley, *Songwriter*

"20 Beautiful Women is a well-written inspirational journey. I was able to relate to each of the women, and each chapter was truly an awakening. This book will inspire you push past your own fears and to pursue your passion and encourage you to never give up."

–Tunda Wannamaker, *Spiritual Life Coach, Alignment Specialist and Truth Seeker*

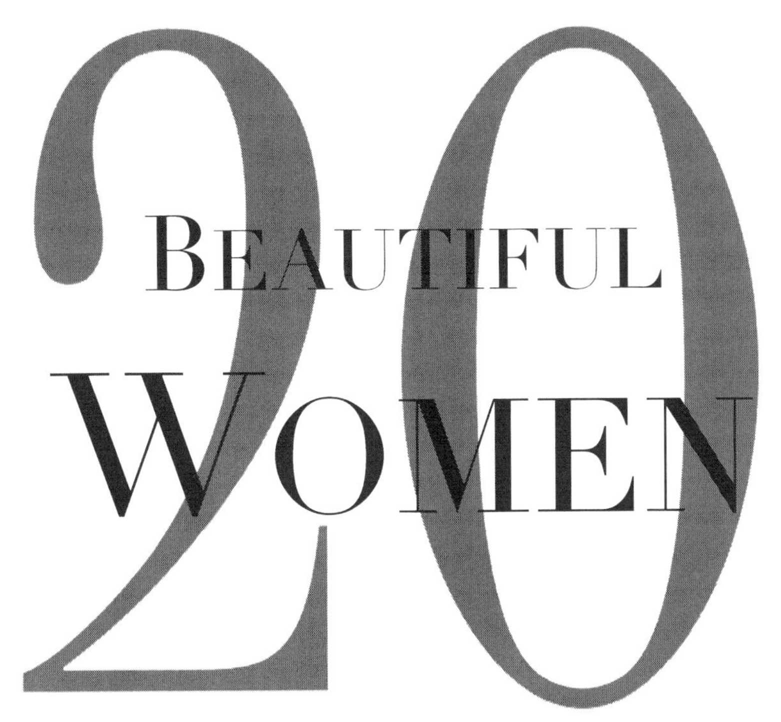

20 STORIES THAT WILL HEAL YOUR SOUL,
IGNITE YOUR PASSION, AND INSPIRE YOUR DIVINE PURPOSE

7 Publishing
www.7-publishing.com
Seattle, Washington

ISBN-13: 978-0692275108
ISBN-10: 069227510X

Book Design by Saba Tekle

Contents

Foreword

By Debrena Jackson Gandy

There is nothing quite like the terrain of the life journey that we uniquely travel as women as we learn, grow, evolve, and most importantly, learn to love and accept ourselves. It is truly a gift when you encounter those who are able to accurately articulate and capture the essence of the challenges, struggles, and triumphs that are part of the "becoming a real woman" process.

In *20 Beautiful Women* you have a collection of such stories – those that chronicle the key lessons, insights, and "aha's" that are a part of our coming of age, wisdom, and maturity as women. It is indeed an art to be able to wrap in words our life experiences, especially those that may have brought us to our knees, taken us to the mountaintop, or blew our minds wide open, to have us never be the same. These stories will touch your heart, soothe your soul, invite you to question what you've come to hold as true, and challenge you to grow.

When you think about the types of topics that are near and dear to the hearts of most women, as we learn along the way, how to shed "who we aren't" for "who we are," there are consistent themes we encounter. Whether it is stories that deal with awakening to your woman power, being extraordinary without fear, overcoming debilitating insecurities, painful lessons learned with money, learning to find your voice, expressing yourself fully without apology, or rediscovering hope after a devastating relationship, *20 Beautiful Women* encourages and empowers you to count it all useful, and to count it all relevant and growth-supporting.

Through this moving anthology of stories, you'll be given intimate glimpses into pivotal moments and turning points in the lives of these incredible women. In each story, you may recognize an aspect of yourself that may enable you to relate to and even better understand parts of the life journey, which you, too, similarly may have traveled. Fresh perspectives, gratitude, new appreciation, liberating release, and a renewed way of thinking are some of what you can expect as you journey through these pages.

As a non-fiction author, I understand how it can stretch a writer to have to take something that she may have shared only in the pages of her diary or journal, or shared intimately with God, and then be willing to convert it into words in a book that she hopes and prays will be a well-received gift, with the desire to see it transform others too. I can feel this same passion arising from the writers as I read through the pages of *20 Beautiful Women.*

For each writer, her life experiences have textured and impacted her life in a way that her life calling is now about supporting and empowering other women to set themselves free from limitations they may have had put on their minds, bodies, and spirits by others, or those that are even self-imposed. These limitations can take the form of emotional baggage from your past, from flawed thinking, from harsh self-judgment, or from self-condemnation or rejection.

Not just any young women, but speakers, coaches, facilitators, and those with the gift of teaching, the writers who have been brought together for this "Beautiful" collaboration are those who are finding their way through the maze-like aspects that life can present, aspects that often are painful, confusing, and hurtful, but always refining. They have emerged clearer, bolder, and more courageous than ever, and invite you to do the same.

You may find yourself shedding a tear, as I did, or saying YES out loud, with a triumphant fist pump as you read these ries. And that is the way it should be.

What were previously dark secrets have been transformed into victory stories so that you can be inspired, uplifted, and encouraged, to fall in love with yourself for the first time, or once again, and instead of "beating yourself up," learning to embrace every perceived imperfection, every flaw that your personal life journey has presented to you and brought you through thus far, without further judgment, comparison, or overly critical analysis.

I can hear the chains breaking, and I can see the doors of too often self-imposed jail cell doors swinging open wide. I see women stepping across the threshold, never to look back or go back to limitation, or self-doubt. *20 Beautiful Women* invites you to shine, shine, shine, and gives you permission to do so, if you need it.

May you see yourself as an even more powerful, beautiful, feminine woman as a result of allowing the words and stories of *20 Beautiful Women* to minister to your soul.

Beauti-FULLY Yours,
Debrena Jackson Gandy

Introduction

By Saba Tekle

Most of my life I lived in pain, and one of my deepest pains was feeling I was alone. When I would open up about my troubles to friends I would either experience them not caring or them sharing what I wanted to keep secret. Although I had family, sometimes I needed someone outside of them to help me. It would leave me feeling like I had no one to turn to, at times, but God. God, I felt, would then guide me to books.

From every book I read from I would get so much healing and relief because of the author's courage and vulnerability to share things that I learned to keep hidden. My beautiful soul and spiritual sisters, Iyana Vanzant, Marianne Williamson, and Lisa Nichol, to name a few, empowered me, taught me so much, and allowed me to see that I was never alone. I began to see that people were just good at masking their pain, and I connected more dots.

Many of us hide parts of our lives, learning early on to tuck the ugly pains away, with hopes that people won't be able to see through us. Like the SPANX we would wear, we put on fake smiles and personalities to camouflage our pains and our flaw-filled lives.

We've learned to look good on the outside while creating the ability to flawlessly hide parts of ourselves. This causes us to die on the inside, and yet, barely existing, we still call this "living." Our souls and spirits wither every day we walk in an inauthentic manner, disillusioned of what a perfect person or perfect life is.

But now, through the mist of darkness and confusion, I have brought nineteen other beautiful women to rise together to shine the light on true beauty. Twenty beautiful women stand naked together, exposing their imperfections, their emotional scars and wounds — wounds that have inspired each of them to be who they are and do the work they do for people today.

A beautiful woman shares her story so other women won't feel alone.
A beautiful woman is peaceful: she has made peace with her past.
A beautiful woman is passionate: she is on fire with a strong desire to change the world.
A beautiful woman is purposeful: she knows why she was born and does what she was created here to do.

Be Beautiful,

Saba Tekle

Chapter 1
Sisterhood

By Danielle Foster

I remember when I first joined the United States Air Force at the age of twenty. Although I grew up in a military family and completed three years of Junior ROTC in high school, I was still quite anxious and a bit nervous about what was up ahead for me on this new journey. This was my first time leaving the nest and experiencing independence, and as I laid there wide awake the night before my flight, I began trying to remind myself of all the reasons why I was making the right decision. However, when morning came I was still stressed as I stepped off the plane and gathered with the group of other recruits. I could feel my body overheating as we got closer and closer to the airbase by nightfall. Thankfully we were allowed one last peaceful slumber in our new quarters before our six weeks of conformity began. I, in all my anxiety, could not sleep longer than twenty minutes at a time, so again I found myself wide awake, reflecting and waiting for the test of my fortitude to begin.

Immediately our training began bright and early and without mercy. There was no more time for second-guessing. In fact, there wasn't much time for anything other than doing what we were told to do. I remember the day we met our training instructor for the first time, a male drill sergeant. All thirty plus of us girls were rushed into the day room and told to sit on the floor in front of him and his all-male staff as they began roll call and assigning various positions to some of us. A number of them were leadership positions, and although I was accustomed to holding quite a few leadership roles throughout my life, in that moment I silently prayed to be hidden and overlooked for any possible hint of leadership and responsibility. I couldn't believe that I was crying out for an opportunity to be a follower! Yet, I couldn't shake my feelings of inadequacy. So I simply prayed to get through the next six weeks as inconspicuously as possible so that I could go on to finishing college and every other aspiration I had. But suddenly I realized after looking around the room that I was the only girl who didn't get the memo about how to get by unnoticed. There I sat with a head full of big curls and a bright blouse. What on earth was I thinking? How could I possibly hide in a sea of women who all wore their hair slicked back in ponytails, no makeup, sweatshirts, and jeans?

I panicked, and before I could cry, I heard my name called out, followed by, "You're the Dorm Chief since you think you can come up in my house and sit on my floor with that damn paint on your face? Go wash it off!" I ran to the restroom, washed the make-up off, and when I returned I discovered that I had just acquired the most important, yet the most daunting responsibility of them all. My drill sergeant explained it this way, "Every mistake you make, you will pay the consequences. Every mistake any of these girls make, you will pay the consequences. Every mistake this flight makes, you will pay the consequences. No mistakes, no consequences. Got it?"

"Yes, sir!" I answered.

The following weeks were totally demanding and uncompromising. My drill sergeant meant every word he spoke to me that day. I paid the price for every mishap in my group, but I can honestly say that although my experiences in Basic Training started in difficulty and tremendous doubt in my ability to lead and perform under extreme pressure, I came out having perfected the art of team building among a group of sister strangers. We were all forced to organize and find a working harmony among us amidst a male-structured environment, but surprisingly we went about accomplishing with excellence the tasks we were given in the most feminine ways.

Things like frequent sister circles right before bed where we got a few minutes to talk about individual difficulties and how we could solve them as a group. Of course these little pow-wows had to be done under the radar as we weren't allowed to do much talking, but conversation is essential for women, and our short discussions are what bonded us in sisterhood. It's what inspired us to look after one another and cover one another when we made a mistake. It's what allowed us to maintain our intuition and connection to each other and being able to sense a weakness in the group and address it by checking up on that fellow sister. It's what kept the cliquish behaviors and spitefulness at bay. Pushed beyond limit with the weight of my sisters' and my own personal weaknesses on my shoulders, I learned in those six weeks what some still struggle to accept, and that is the fact that women are absolutely capable of success in leadership and organizational roles. When we are given the opportunity to lead as women and without the expectation to lead as men, we thrive.

There's one experience that for me greatly defined the power of the feminine essence of leadership, transparency, and transformation and will forever stay in my memory. It was on this particular night that I found myself in the dormitory restroom crying with and consoling a fellow sister who had become sick and had just found out that she was pregnant by her boyfriend back at home. She was terrified! She wanted so badly to get through the following weeks, but all she could think about was the baby growing inside of her along with her worst fear – that she would be forced to raise her baby alone when she returned home, all of which left her with the agonizing temptation to have an abortion as soon as she got through Basic Training. I can't remember what moved her to open up to me about her dilemma, as I was sure I was wearing the stress of my own role as Dorm Chief on my face from sun up to sun down, but whatever it was that inspired her to vulnerability, I am grateful for it. It was in the middle of this night as we sat there alone that she and I were changed forever.

After listening to her pain and wiping away her tears, I began to share with her my own testimony of a time when I was sixteen and dating a man five years older than me. It was in this relationship, my very first courtship, that I not only lost my virginity, but had gotten pregnant by that first encounter. Yes, sixteen and pregnant! That was me, less than four years ago at the time that I allowed myself to share in her vulnerability. I told her that at sixteen I could not fathom what this experience would mean for me. But I was willing to take that journey – that is, until I discovered that I would have to take it alone. When I gave the news to my boyfriend, he panicked. In fact, the news agitated him so much so that he told me for the first time about a girl in another city that was the mother of his son. He proceeded to plead with me over an abortion, which I had never heard of. When he described to me with little detail what an abortion was, I just hung up the phone and cried. I was so dizzy from confusion and felt so empty and alone.

A couple of days later on my ride home from school with a friend, I decided to inquire what she knew about pregnancy and abortions. To my astonishment she nonchalantly shared that she had just had one last summer and that it wasn't as bad as she thought it'd be. According to her it was an in and out procedure, some blood and some cramping, but nothing major, and that if I could get $325 she would take me to the clinic and no one would ever have to know. No one knowing was a big concern, but getting $325 with no job was an even bigger one. It seemed like such a difficult task and only ended up spiraling me deeper into my already growing depression.

As my breasts grew larger and my favorite perfumes and foods threw me into the worst episodes of nausea, I remember getting a phone call one evening and hearing a voice I didn't recognize. She asked if she was speaking to Danielle and I said yes. I then asked who I was speaking to. She introduced herself by first name and without warning instantly began going off about me being with her man and how she was the mother of his son and was currently pregnant with his second child. I wanted to vomit. She continued to rant as I just sat there with hot tears streaming from my eyes. When she finally calmed down and realized that I wasn't putting up a fight, she asked about me. I told her where I was from, that I had just found out that I was pregnant by the same guy, that I had no idea whatsoever that he had a girlfriend, let alone a family, and that she didn't have to worry about me because we just broke up over his pressuring me about an abortion. She asked me how old I was and when I told her, she let out a wail, one similar to what I expected from my mother if I was ever forced to tell her what was happening to her baby girl.

After she finished crying loudly, the woman on the other line began to apologize to me. She told me that I was just a child and that she was currently twenty years old, but was seventeen when she had her first son. She began to tell me that before she met him she was a ballet dancer. She had aspirations to graduate high school and continue her studies in choreography, but she too had gotten pregnant at an early age and though she still thought about going to school, she was currently struggling to take care of the child she had and was worried about the one on the way. I told her about my dreams to become a nurse and she seemed so happy to hear that. We talked about a few other things and even though she was four years older than me, I found myself at times encouraging her. Her last words to me were to never give up on whatever I aspired to do in life. She made me promise her that I wouldn't allow any circumstances to stop me from pursuing my dreams. I made her that promise and we hung up as sisters, probably never to hear from each other again in this lifetime.

It was this testimony that I mustered up what little courage I had to share with my fellow sister that night in the hallway of our dorm while the rest of our sisters slept. I had never told anyone outside of my mother, my close friend in high school, and the few people involved about my pregnancy and my abortion, but something was happening to me as I heard the fear and hopelessness in my sister's voice. She needed to know that she was not alone in her feelings or in her circumstance. It was my mustard seed faith to open my heart and share an experience that even I was still healing from that transformed the both of us that night.

My testimony of the shame I felt, the betrayal I experienced, the physical pain of the abortion, the years of depression that followed, and the emotional anguish that still haunts me, all had a huge impact on her decision. But I think it was the transparency of our vulnerability that bonded us in true sisterhood. This sister of mine graduated Basic Training with all of us and today enjoys the blessing of her son, who she chose to keep because of our encounter.

Biography:

Danielle Foster is a dynamic inspirational writer, community organizer, activist, life coach, and certified personal trainer whose focus in self-mastery and holistic health, nutrition and fitness education has encouraged many to embrace the concept of loving ourselves first. She is also a veteran of the United States Air Force, having served over a decade as an Aerospace Medical Technician and EMT instructor. As a leader in her community, she has worked alongside some of the most influential motivational speakers, including former NFL player, Trent Shelton, of RehabTime©.

Contact Information:
www.facebook.com/daniellfosterinspires
www.twitter.com/EarthSoul7
danielleFosterInspires@gmail.com

Chapter 2
An Abortion of Insecurities
By Jennifer Wilkes

Since I was a little girl I knew that one day I wanted to be married. Having that profound lifetime connection with someone was important to me. I grew up witnessing the beautiful ups and crazy downs of my parents' forty-four year marriage. Although I saw the interactions between them, I still didn't quite understand how to set standards in my own relationships. Yes, I wanted honesty and loyalty, but how could I really have those things sincerely from a man? I was always trying to figure out what was wrong with my boyfriend or what was wrong with me. Why was I not enough for him? Why was there always another woman who was a factor in my relationship? Why was it so easy for me to be transparent and loyal, but not so simple for him? Were all men essentially the same? I was constantly fighting emotional battles, and I didn't understand how to cope. With each relationship I left feeling like I had wasted my time, but there was one that left me with more disappointment than any of the others.

After graduating from high school I decided to attend Voorhees College two hours away from home. During my freshman year in college I tutored one of my biology classmates. He was a basketball player that I used to see at the parties on campus. I first noticed him because he was a really good dancer, and I loved to dance. He was rather attractive too. At the time I had just come out of a relationship with a guy I was dating back at home in Florence, so I was in a very vulnerable place. His humor was addictive, and his charm was easily convincing.

During some of our sessions I confided in him about my previous relationship. We became close and eventually ended up dating, or at least that's what I thought. Most of the time he was busy avoiding his ex-girlfriend while we were together because he didn't want her to see us. For instance, he would casually walk away from me if he saw her car pulling up. Sometimes he gave me excuses on why he couldn't attend a school event with me because he knew she would be there. He told me she was jealous, which she may have been, but I didn't see the reason for us to hide our relationship because of it. By this time it should've occurred to me that maybe he was telling me and her different things, but it didn't. I was trying to stay in love by focusing on his better qualities. The emotional rollercoaster had just begun. Little did I know that there were going to be many loops ahead that I had yet to encounter.

The situation with his ex became annoying. I remember thinking, *If she wasn't in the way, our relationship would be close to perfect.* I gave him chance after chance, one ultimatum after another to make it clear to her that we were in a relationship, but to no avail. There were many signs that I needed to leave him alone. One minute he wanted to be with me, and the next minute he needed time to think. We were up, then down, but I held on with hopes that things would change. However, I had no clue that within a year my life would change entirely.

His ex graduated and I was relieved that we wouldn't have to deal with that issue next year. It was supposed to be smooth coasting for us to enjoy being together, so I thought. But after starting my second year in college, I found out I was pregnant. Even though we were now in a good place, he wasn't too excited about it, and I couldn't blame him. We were both trying to finish school. Not to mention, I was a musician at my church. I knew that being unwed and pregnant wasn't going to sit well with everyone, especially my parents. To ease the religious tension, we got engaged. Even though our relationship wasn't consistently stable, we knew we wanted to marry each other eventually. So, why not?

I told my mom first, and surprisingly, she wasn't upset. She told me she knew I would handle my responsibilities and finish school. He and I told my dad together. I saw the disappointment on his face, but he didn't get upset. He stayed calm, but was firm in questioning us on our plans for the baby and our relationship. We assured him we would get married after we finished college. Though my parents handled the news well, I knew that having a baby in college wasn't part of their plans for me. I didn't think it was the best time for me to be having a baby, but I had no choice except to face the reality.

At the end of the semester I transferred to a school in my hometown and forfeited my full scholarship. Part of me was disappointed, but I knew it was best for me to go back home. All in all, it wasn't too disheartening because I was still able to stay in school, be with my family, and allow my mom to spoil me with her cooking. It was in my DNA to keep moving ahead no matter what. No possible excuse was going to stop me from doing what I had initially set out to do.

My fiancé wanted to transfer with me, but he had to stay at the school because of financial obligations. I didn't see him as much. Some weekends he would catch a ride to come see me. Then there were other weekends I expected him to come, and he just wouldn't show up. No call. Nothing. There were times he didn't answer his phone, and I had to call around campus just to get in touch with him. He would find every excuse as to why he couldn't make it. We argued often, and sometimes I screamed at him that he couldn't see the baby once she was born because of his foolishness.

Why did he not want to see me? Why was I chasing after him when he was showing me that he didn't want to be with me? Many questions clouded my mind, and they never seemed to cease. I cried more and more, passing my sadness to my womb, but I did feel like he loved me...sometimes. Plus, he was handsome. He was funny. He could dance, and it wasn't like we never got along. We had many great times together. Why not stay and stick it out for our baby? So I stayed. We tried to push through, but this back-and-forth between us continued well after my daughter was born.

Not long after my daughter turned two, the rollercoaster of life brought me to an unexpected drop. I was at my parents' house while he was at work and the doorbell rang. When I opened the door, there stood a sheriff holding one of those large gold envelopes. She stated his name and asked if this was a contact address for him. I said, "Yes," and she handed it to me and left. Initially, I thought maybe he had put himself on child support. We'd had some arguments recently, and I had given him some space, but why would the envelope be addressed to him? It wasn't sealed so I opened it. What I found in that envelope made my heart race for what seemed like a million times a second. They were, in fact, child support papers, but not for my daughter. In the most insensitive way I found out he had fathered another child a year after our daughter was born.

It felt like I had shed most of the tears in my body that day. Betrayal, foolishness, and heartache ran through my body. I was devastated. It was a blatant slap in my face, and to make matters worse, he denied it all until he was forced to tell the truth with a DNA test months later. Our relationship had come full circle. The lies and deception were now blatantly obvious.

After learning the DNA results, I had a revelation. Who was I going to be for my daughter? What was I going to demonstrate for her about womanhood? There was no way I could still marry him. I was no longer the same woman. I looked in the mirror and faced myself. Not only was I insecure about who I was, but the men I dated were insecure about who they were. I was never in a relationship with them. I was dating their insecurities while trying to tackle my own. Not to dismiss his actions or those of other men I dated, but I was in denial. Until that point, my identity was somewhat defined by relationships with men instead of a relationship with myself. No longer could I blame someone else for what I had allowed to happen in my life. There was no one who could rescue me from my own insecurities but myself. I've been told that I was lucky to grow up having parents who were still together. Some people believe that having two parents in the household solves most of life's problems, but for me, that wasn't always true. Yes, they were there to support me and love me, but they weren't able to relate to what I was going through. They've had each other for over half of their lifetimes. What I experienced as a single mom was somewhat foreign to them. But they gave me unwavering support.

There were no classes that could've ever prepared me for the challenges that came with being a single mom. Being a single mom didn't happen to me; it happened for me. It gave me the opportunity to learn how to embrace whatever comes into my life and let go of the picture perfect fantasies. Life wasn't always going to go the way I wanted it to, but it would always happen the way it needed to.

After all I went through, I realized that I never wasted my time in any relationship. Each relationship prepared me for who I needed to be. I needed to learn how to love myself more, undeniably. My daughter needed to see a woman who was in love with herself first. Motherhood pushed me beyond limits that I would have never thought I could face. Having my daughter gave me the chance to redefine who I wanted to be. I began to see myself differently. I was now a parent who was responsible for demonstrating the essence of life and love to my daughter. Having her inspired me to transform my values. No longer was I going to settle for a mediocre life and mediocre relationships. The bitter-sweetness of motherhood was my rite of passage into a beautiful womanhood.

Biography:

Jennifer Wilkes is a communication and leadership coach from Florence, South Caroline. With a mission to serve, she created COLD Consulting (Communication, Organizational and Leadership Development) and coaches entrepreneurs, families, and students. She believes in the power of effective leadership and understands the importance of communication in all areas of life. Her unique and direct approach has motivated many to overcome personal and professional challenges. Some clients have coined her "The COLD Coach."

Jennifer has experience in radio, print journalism, public relations, and corporate communications. She holds a BA in Mass Communication with a minor in Gender Studies from Francis Marion University. She completed her MA in Communication and Leadership Studies from Gonzaga University and received a certificate in International Media while studying abroad in Italy.

Jennifer is a firm believer that leaders have the duty to produce other leaders, and her ultimate mission is to help others become leaders of their own lives.

Contact Information:
www.TheCOLDcoach.com
Jennifer@thecoldconsultant.com
P.O. Box 94596
Atlanta, GA 30377

Chapter 3

An Autobiography of a Modern Day Yogi

By Tejal Patel

My story is one of a child, a young adult, and then a woman living life with a deep underlying fear —the fear of becoming my mother. I didn't want to manipulate others by throwing fits of emotional rage and I didn't want to bring children into the world unless I could give them the emotional, physical, AND spiritual attention they deserved.

Being a sensitive child I internalized my mother's anger, pain, and insecurity. My non-confrontational, peace striving father would tell me, "Sometimes you have to apologize, even when it's not your fault to smooth things over and make your mom calm down." Trying to bring peace by adjusting my behavior to assuage my mother's anger came at a large price; The inhibition of my emotional expression, repression of negative emotions, and disconnection to my inner voice.

From a young age I was constantly nervous around my mother. I was walking on eggshells making sure I said and did the right thing so my mother wouldn't get angry. The constant dialogue in my mind was "Will my mom get mad?" Many times I walked away unscathed by her anger, but sometimes I would unintentionally do something to trigger an emotional outburst from her. I was tiptoeing around a time bomb, trying to avoid the next catastrophic emotional explosion.

As a teenager, starving for authentic emotional nurturance and wanting my feelings to be acknowledged began my ploy for attention. My parents "you have to do as I say, without questioning, because I'm older and know more" rationale no longer worked. I was tired of being controlled, scared, and apologizing when it wasn't my fault. My battered ego finally found its voice and my parents and I engaged in a battle of the supremacy of egos. Becoming a defiant and disconnected teenager, I would avoid talking to my parents for days, would lie to minimize conflict, and experimented with alcohol, at the age of sixteen to numb my pain. Their rigidness, lack of trust, and inability to connect pushed me further away. Gone were the days of the sweet, innocent, and complacent daughter. I stepped into a new role, the angry and wounded young woman.

As I entered college with a wounded heart, I strived to fill my emotional void by seeking love, approval, and attention from men. It was in my romantic relationships that a harsh reality came forth. I would unintentionally manipulate my boyfriends to get the self-worth I wasn't willing to give myself. When my boyfriends didn't meet my expectations I would have similar anger outbursts like my mother, until I got the response I was seeking.

How did this happen? Despite my resistance, I was becoming like my mother. I was filled with insecurity, consumed by fear, and seeking validation. The drama I created was a result of my inability to tolerate the pain from my unhealed childhood. I would either run from my feelings through avoidance or if they resurfaced, I would project my anger onto other people and external situations by blaming others and not taking responsibility for my emotions.

I created a false image of being perfect, intelligent, bubbly, and cheerful to hide the angry and wounded girl inside. Feeling exhausted from keeping up an inauthentic facade, drinking each weekend was my escape and the only time I could let my guard down. I numbed all the uncomfortable emotions I was too afraid to confront. In my mid 20's, drinking no longer had the same luster as it did in college. With each drink I would sink into a spiral of self-loathing and my childhood pain became too unbearable to be repressed by alcohol.

At twenty-five, the external sources that I believed would bring me happiness, my beauty, money, credentials, law career and relationships, only brought me emptiness. The inauthentic life I had worked so hard to sustain shattered open, and I hit rock bottom. Waking from the haze of a hangover, feeling alone, disconnected, and directionless, I surrendered to my suffering and begged for help. At that time I wasn't religious or spiritual, but I did believe there was a greater divine force. For three days I laid in bed alone, hysterically crying, and desperately asked whomever was watching over me "I've completely lost control over my life, someone please help me."

Within a short time, the Universe sent me my first saving grace: *The Secret.* This began the first phase of my spiritual journey: acquiring spiritual wisdom. Restoring my hope that I had power to change my life, I began acknowledging and shifting my negative thoughts and beliefs. I received guidance from books, authors, and blogs that helped me learn the truth of my identity and how to tap into my inner world to find peace. Thus began a five-year journey to learn about metaphysical principles, understanding the fundamentals of compassion, forgiveness and love through religious texts, healing myself through Reiki and practicing Kundalini Yoga and Meditation to unblock past patterns and reconnecting to my inner voice.

The journey of reconnecting to my inner voice required me to delve into my childhood pain. Until I healed my anger towards my mom, released the need to seek validation from my parents and reframed my "victim" story so I could let go of my past, my emotional pain would continue to be re-triggered by present relationships, friendships, and eventually my future children.

As I opened up to spiritual concepts, I knew the level of pain and attachment my mom and I experienced must stem from relationships spanning beyond this lifetime. I was guided to do past life regression hypnosis to understand the soul journeys my mom and I had taken together, to bring us to this lifetime. It was from understanding our joint spiritual lessons, our previous relationships, and the pain we had been carrying around for many lifetimes, I was finally able to understand my mother and find compassion for her soul.

No matter how much my ego tried to convince my mother to apologize for her actions, it was only when I released my ego and saw my mother as a soul first and my mother second, I was able to let go and forgive. For someone to have so much anger, I recognized she had a broken, wounded girl within her, just like me.

I'd taken on the role of the "victim" in my mind, which perpetuated the discord in our relationship. Rather than expecting my mom to change and apologize first, I took the initiative. I openly expressed my emotions, apologized for my part and forgave her with the intention to start fresh. Over time, she recognized and apologized for her past mistakes. I reclaimed my power by no longer holding my mother responsible for my pain and believing happiness is an inside job, a choice I make.

Once I forgave my mom, then came the second phase of my spiritual journey: a disciplined spiritual practice. As an adult, though I released the pain of the past, I still absorbed the negativity and low level energy of my parents, friends, and my divorcing law clients. Being around arguing clients re-triggered my childhood anxiety. The tension and heavy emotions drained my energy and caused me to react from a space of impatience and anger. Though I forgave my mother, the negative patterns still had their roots within. I needed tools to help me avoid absorbing other people's negative baggage and start becoming responsible for how my negative reactions affected others.

I was introduced to yoga and meditation to cope with my anger and anxiety. Through Kundalini meditations, I broke negative habits that no longer served me, raised my energy vibrations, and felt inner peace. I began to wander if I would have better expressed my emotions and not internalized my childhood pain if I knew these tools at a young age.

At twenty-nine, I started the third phase of my spiritual journey: following my calling to inspire others to awaken to their inner truth. I had a deep knowing that my life purpose would not be fulfilled by advocating human laws in a courtroom, but rather by advocating universal spiritual laws to adults so they could interact with future generations from a more awakened space. Determined to use the insights I gained from my challenging childhood lessons, I was motivated to teach children how to cope with difficult life circumstances and emotions.

This was my driving force to leave my career as an attorney and get certified as a children's yoga and meditation instructor. I teach children intuition connection, expressing emotions, conscious breathing, and positive self-image. I plant the seeds of mindfulness to empower children to calmly deal with life's fears, anxiety, and stress.

My calling expanded to empower children and inspire adults to awaken to their own inner power. Through my life coaching, articles, and weekly Astitva Seeker Vlogs, I teach adults how to cultivate inner peace and tap into their higher self so they can be a better example for their families. As parents begin tuning into their inner compass, they will find more direction in their life and thus build a greater connection with their children. It is my life mission to make yoga and meditation easy and accessible, so families can practice together. Because of my family experiences, I understand the value of families growing and bonding together and how yoga and meditation facilitates deep healing and spiritual connections.

Now in my 30's, as I prepare for my own journey toward motherhood, I look back at my childhood and mother with love, appreciation, and compassion. My most challenging relationship has served to be the greatest blessing, because it cracked me open to heal deep wounds that followed us for many lifetimes.

Despite our parents' best intentions, they don't maliciously hurt us. It's not their lack of love, but their lack of connection to their own inner spirit that prevents them from connecting to their children's unique spirit. If parents are not taught how to awaken to become the best version of themselves, they are unable to model that for their children. The fear of emulating our parents' negative traits becomes a reality, unless we consciously let our intuitive inner voice guide us.

As an adult I've re-defined my relationship with my parents. The growth of a family is one of spiritual partnerships, not parents being the superior and the child being the less than. Each soul is bonded together as a spiritual teacher for the other, while still being an independent person, having their own unique spiritual calling, lessons, and destiny. As our parents spiritual guides, it's through understanding their suffering, forgiving their mistakes, and having compassion, that we help them learn from their mistakes, heal their deepest fears, and spiritually grow.

I now have a new story. I am a radiant spiritual teacher, empowered woman, and light worker committed to bring greater awareness, peace, and healing to the world. I am grateful for the challenging relationship I had with my mother, for it helped me stop the cycle of anger and feel the urgency to awaken and take a spiritual path at a young age. I reinvented my life to become a better human being, a conscious mother, and dedicated spiritual teacher to inspire others to tap into their higher self. I transcended to these great heights so early in my life because I consciously transformed my suffering into a positive spiritual experience.

Biography:

Tejal Patel is a former divorce attorney and mediator who reinvented her life to become a children's yoga instructor, spiritual life coach, motivational speaker, and writer. She teaches Kundalini yoga and meditation techniques to help parents develop a stronger relationship with themselves and their families. She coaches clients around the world to guide them on their own spiritual awakening journey.

Contact Information:
www.astitvaseekers.com
www.yogabirdies.com.

Chapter 4
Stepping-Stones to Healing
By Dawn Allen

As a child, I remember being at family reunions, observing my family appearing to be normal and full of love. I felt like the black sheep because of the abuse I experienced at home, so I would seclude myself by hiding in my Grandmother's closet. Secretly I craved being around everyone, but in her wardrobe I felt safe from any hurt and pain from others.

Behind closed doors, my house was no home. It was filled with mental, physical, and sexual abuse. Once I ran to my mother, after hearing her screaming, to witness my father beating her like a man. I attempted to help her by grabbing his arm, and he hit me so hard my body flew across the room.

As I grew up, I witnessed the physical abuse turn deadly. Their cycle of him beating her, them breaking up, then getting back together, which was toxic, was at its breaking point. With every cycle, it got worse, and the death threats turned into nights filled with rage and a count down to who would go first.

My mother packed up our things to leave him and moved to my Grandmother's. While she was driving back to grab more things, my father was following her, threatening to burn down the house. My mother took his threats seriously, and it grew so intense that it turned into a car race to the gun kept in the house. My father rammed into my mother's car with his car in an attempt to beat her to the gun but lost.

She grabbed it, shot two warning shots, and pleaded with him to stop, but my father persisted to attack her. She shot him twice, and my father died three times on the way to the hospital. Eventually he made it, but it left him paralyzed and unable to hurt us anymore.

While the physical abuse became very public at that point, sexual abuse lingered privately that left me hating everyone. I was molested and raped consistently by my biological dad, until my body, soul, and mind would go numb. Then I was threatened by my father; he would say if I told, somebody would get hurt or that no one would believe me.

I believed him, and the hate growing inside me was like a wildfire that couldn't be contained from what I experienced. Since I had no one to go to, I became rebellious. I would lash out at my mother by being very disrespectful. I would use foul language and run away a lot. I would even throw rocks at her. In a strange way, I was upset at her for shooting my dad. Oddly, I was mad that she hurt my abuser and because I felt that I couldn't tell her all the things that were happening during the weekend court ordered visits to my dad's.

She would try disciplining me by hitting me until she was exhausted; sometimes she'd choke me until I was breathless. Every day was filled with fights that left me drained mentally and emotionally. Filled with despair, emptiness and loneliness, eventually this lead to my first attempt suicide.

I didn't want to kill myself, just the pain.

Before then, overdosing on pills was a daily thought that I never acted on. Then one day I woke up in a hospital, unsuccessful in my attempt.

Immediately after I was put in a psych ward where I had mandatory group therapy sessions with other suicidal men and en. During these sessions, 90% of them revealed they had been sexually abused and hearing that turned into the beginning of my first breakthrough. Before this, I thought I was the only one going through this. It gave me the courage finally to tell my mom.

Telling my mom started to release the pain inside me that wanted to be released. She believed me and she had even approached my father and told him, "If you ever touch her again I will finish what I started." But not too long after, I felt the pain lock back up with something heavier covering it. I attempted another suicide; this time I wanted to die.

When I recovered, I was right back in the psych ward. I went under a lot of evaluations again, but I still had no one to relate to because the counselors and therapists I encountered had knowledge based off of books and not experience. I was told to do certain things a certain way and things would get better ... well guess what? That was far from the truth. This time I finally made a friend who was also my roommate, Cathy. She was an older lady that had also experienced similar things to what I was going through. She was the first person I felt comfortable with confiding in deeply. I told her everything in detail from the places the abuse happened to how it happened. We continued to stay in touch after we got out of the hospital, and she eventually helped me run away. She paid someone to take me to her house a few hours away from my home. There she had a daughter and son several years younger than myself, and they felt like the family I wanted but never had. I was gone for maybe one month, and it caused such a stir that my mother had a nervous breakdown. But being with Cathy gave me peace and relief I had never felt because I was safe from harm with her.

State troopers picked me up, and I was immediately put into foster care. During this process, my mom sat in front of a judge to have her rights removed because she couldn't control me, and my two suicide attempts revealed an unstable home. I became a ward of the state, and Cathy was forbidden from contacting me. I felt more alone then ever felt before.

In my first home, some of the foster kids and I were isolated. We weren't allowed to eat at the table during family dinners. Most of the "outcast" foster kids were given leftovers and made to eat cold food if the "chosen" kids wanted to take longer to finish dinner. I knew this wasn't right or normal, but I wasn't normal so I thought that experiencing this was just another nail in the coffin.

Being in this home, I felt a sixth sense develop. For some reason, I realized I had a strange gift; I can pick up whether or not someone has been sexually abused.

Walking into the home of people that were supposed to be my caretakers, I felt extremely uncomfortable, and chills would run down my spine in their presence. I knew something wasn't right, but this time I wasn't the victim.

Fortunately, I still had relatives that cared. They requested for me to be moved closer to the area near them. I was moved to a foster home with a family that were devoted Christians in the same county as my family members. It was a good, bad, happy, and sad transition, and very overwhelming to say the least. When I was away, it was easy to leave behind the pain and problems, but now that I was back, everything I had left behind picked back up.

One day, I tried to suffocate myself by putting a black plastic bag over my head, and the lady that took me in removed it and talked to me about God. I wasn't trying to hear her, but she planted a seed in me that sprouted later in my life.

I was moved again, but this time a distant relative adopted me. I was taken in by my dad's cousin and his wife and kids, They were wonderful to me, but I still managed to turn to drinking and drugs to ease the pain I still had inside. I felt I was only existing in a shell, felt that I had no soul and no heart, yet I still wanted someone to love and wanted to be loved. I met a girl in 10th grade that I become very close with, as well as her family. The Atha's took me in as one of their own, and from there, they started taking me to church. There I heard many teachings on forgiveness.

Time passed and I met a guy – my high school sweetheart – that I wanted to spend every waking minute with. Then at the age of 16, I found out I was pregnant. In my last trimester, the physical abuse began to surface. It didn't take long before I experienced the same cycle my mother had been in. The abuse of being hit, spit on, choked, squeezed so hard that I couldn't breathe, verbally abused to the point that I felt I deserved the physical abuse, and at times even forced to have sex.

The cycle turned me into the "girl who cried wolf". Family members grew tired of my issues, and it was mostly because I would go back to him. It was because I wanted my boys to have a daddy; at times he was charming and I wanted to be with him. But I had officially hit rock bottom. One day an argument escalated from inside our home to out in the streets. Shortly, he had started beating my head on a neighbor's car. While this was happening, I looked at my front door and I saw my three little boys looking out at us, my oldest looked dead at me while I was being beaten. I then ran and called the cops. Within seconds, I heard the cops coming. That day he was taken to jail and told to stay away from the house, myself and our boys.

That was the last straw. I had nowhere to turn to but God. The seeds that had been planted from my foster parent and going to church with the Atha's where beginning to sprout and so I began to pray. I prayed aloud sometimes while crying, asking tirelessly, *what do I do? Where do I go?* until I'd fall asleep. I wanted so badly for things to be better, peaceful, and normal, so I kept praying and reading my bible until the answer, eventually, was to forgive.

1st: I started with forgiving my mother and father for the physical, mental, emotional, and sexual abuse.

2nd: Then I forgave those I've helped who had turned around and hurt me – even those who wouldn't or couldn't help me.

3rd: Lastly, I had to forgive myself for not taking responsibly for most of my decisions.

From this the biggest peace came over me. I was still challenged when I went to my parents to tell them I had forgiven them.

I walked into my mother's house after I knew from much praying that the timing was right. As we sat down at her kitchen table, I started to tell her all of the hurt and pain I felt, which she had caused me, and how I had so much resentment and anger that I'd been carrying around for years. As my mother and I wept together, I looked her in the eyes and told her, "I forgive you."

But when I went to see my father, the only thing that came out of his mouth was, "It was your mother's fault". He had pushed me to my breaking point, but I knew I had two choices: go back to being angry and that could be the death of me, or continue to forgive him. I chose to forgive.

Forgiving isn't easy, but it's crucial to healing. If you don't forgive, it still gives the person the right to control you mentally and emotionally. When you forgive, you take their power away, and take your own power back. That is where the stepping-stones to healing begin. Healing or forgiving is not forgetting what happened or about restoring the relationship; it about restoring yourself and your life.

Biography:

Dawn Allen is currently happily married, mother of many (four biological), a foster parent, and Court Appointed Special Advocate (CASA) volunteer. She is an author, mentor, and motivational speaker. Dawn uses her experiences to help children of all ages express the challenges they are facing.

Contact Information:
www.dawnberryallen.com

Chapter 5
Pain to Power

By Ashley Cooper

For most of my life, I struggled to see my beauty. In fact, I could barely look at myself in the mirror. Though I tried to make myself more attractive on the outside, it could never cover up how ugly I felt on the inside. It took me years of depression, self-hatred and suicide attempts to realize that beauty is not in the size you wear or in the color of your skin – true beauty comes from within.

There was a short period, until the age of seven, when I remember feeling flawlessly beautiful. Though short-lived, it was a time when labels and the idea of perfection didn't exist to me. It was early on in public school when things began to change. I became the victim of severe bullying, which robbed me of my innocence almost overnight. I think that it was my meekness coupled with my sincere desire to be liked that made me a target. I was never the kind of kid that knew how to stand up for herself and some kids could sense that. There wasn't a day that went by in the early years of public school without some sort of verbal or emotional abuse. I was constantly ridiculed and called things like "stupid" and "ugly". It was the first time in my life that I began thinking that I wasn't good enough just as I was.

By grade seven, things went from bad to worse. My lack of self-love left me with no sense of boundaries. I had become close friends with a girl named Julie and though things started off great, they quickly escalated into serious emotional and at times physical abuse. Although Julie seemed to have a good heart, she had a rough up-bringing that made her take it out on others. Her lack of self-love left her with a deep sense of jealousy toward others, myself in particular. I could feel a sense of competition and conflict growing within her as our friendship developed. Over the course of a year, she became extremely territorial over our friendship and my attention. She began to isolate me from what friends I did have and school became a living hell. She manipulated situations and turned people against me. It even got to the point where my sisters and I were getting threats on our lives from a local gang.

It was a tough time, to say the least. Though my parents begged the school to put an end to the bullying, they were told repeatedly that there was nothing they could do. I began to believe the horrible things that she said and became so ashamed of who I was that I hated myself. I tried so hard to be perfect but nothing I did was ever good enough. I became a prisoner, not only to our friendship, but also to the prison of perfection that I had created in my mind. Though I felt alone, I was too scared to tell anyone in fear that they too would see how worthless I was. Eventually I fell so deep into the hole of depression that suicide attempts and self-mutilation were commonplace. I had cuts running up and down my arm so high that I wore long-sleeved shirts constantly so that no one would notice. I desperately tried to keep up the façade of what I thought it meant to be perfect, but the charade was exhausting. No matter how hard I tried, or how good things looked on the outside, on the inside I was fighting for my life.

After eighth grade graduation, a seeming miracle occurred. The girl who had been bullying me for over two years moved out of the country. The sad thing was that the damage was already done; no bully on earth could ever measure up to how I had come to treat myself. I was so desperate to escape the war within that I became determined to find a solution. I entered high school with a determination to seek out healthier and better friendships. I read as many books as I could get my hands on about empowerment and self-love. Though there were many ups and downs throughout those years, I could feel myself getting stronger and stronger.

In 2000, a year after my High School Graduation I set off to have a fresh start. I attended Lasalle College for Fashion Design in Montreal, hours away from my hometown in Ontario. It was so good to be out on my own, independent and for once loving school. But, in December 2002, things took a turn for the worst. I was out celebrating the end of exams before Christmas with one of my best friends, when I went from sober to drunk really fast. I decided that I needed to take off early and offered to put myself in a cab so as not to ruin everyone else's night. While waiting for a cab, I was approached by one of my guy friends who I secretly had a crush on. He offered to help me home, as I was quite obviously incapacitated. Once arriving at my apartment, the night took a horrific turn. I never thought in a million years that things would end in rape. Afterward, I can just remember lying there in a comatose-like state of shock, pain, and disbelief. As the months passed, the weight of his body against mine became a permanent weight in my life. It didn't take long before the voice of self-hatred returned. Thoughts like, "It's my fault" and "I should have known better" replayed like a broken record in my mind.

Though it had been years since I had considered suicide, I felt desperate, helpless, and out of control. I was emotionally exhausted and once again too ashamed to ask for help. But when I was about to take my life, a voice reached of the darkness and said, *"You have a purpose. You have a mission. Hold on. Keep fighting. Your salvation is coming."*

The voice resonated from the deepest part of me. I believe that it was divine intervention, a true triumph of love over fear. In that very moment, I knew that not only could I save my own life, but perhaps my story could save someone else's. The shift of focus from self to others gave me a new faith and made me more driven than ever before to find a solution. It was a matter of life or death, not just for me, but for others as well.

From that moment on, I decided that I wanted to travel, find myself and heal my past completely. It was a calling more than a decision, almost like I didn't have a choice in the matter. Though I had no idea where I would go, I made a promise to myself that I would let my spirit be my guide. I became determined to choose my destination based on a sign, and within two weeks, my sign arrived. I was out for dinner one night with a friend when our waitress, Becky, appeared distraught. We asked her what was wrong and she said, *"I was supposed to fly to Australia with my best friend, but she cancelled on me at the last minute. I am so scared to fly and travel alone; I need someone to go with "* That was the sign I needed. I had met Becky once or twice before and thought that she would be a fantastic travel companion. Much to her disbelief, I let her know right on the spot that I was the woman for the job. I worked like crazy for a couple of months, took what little money I had and bought myself a one-way ticket to Australia and off Becky and I went.

Though I had never traveled before and was a bit scared, I knew that I was on my life's path, and that's all that mattered. After a couple of months in Sydney, Becky and I decided to split up and go on separate adventures. My journey lead me up the East Coast of Australia, where I deepened my yoga practice and had my first foray into meditation. I met incredible people, stayed with amazing families, and began to love and trust myself for the first time in years. By the end of my year in Australia, I had developed a nagging feeling that I was meant to be in South East Asia. In honor of my promise to follow my soul, I scraped together what money I had and bought a ticket to Thailand. Once in Thailand, I deepened my spiritual practice. I became a Reiki master, studied Tai Qi, Qi Gong, yoga and did whatever I could do to end my suffering.

The most life-changing experience of all was when I took a 21-day vow of silence. A vow of silence is when you make a decision to remove yourself from your normal stimuli such as talking, eating certain foods, interaction with others etc. This is usually paired with hours of meditation and contemplation for the purpose of raising awareness within oneself. I was inspired by the Thai Buddhist Monks, their practice and serenity, and decided to undertake a vow of my own. After the first seven days, I swore I was going to go crazy. The multitude of voices collided in my head and fought for my attention. I felt like I was literally slipping into insanity listening to the chaos in my mind. Then on the seventh day, the inner noise ended abruptly and I was consumed by silence. There was no voice, no anxiety, no fear, no inner chaos, just total and complete inner-peace and stillness. What was even more amazing was that, despite having worn the same few outfits for months and wearing no makeup, I felt more beautiful than I ever had. It was like I was radiating love from the inside out. This experience made an impression on my life that I will never forget. It showed me that beneath the voice of fear and self-hatred laid a deep sense of love. It is from this place that true beauty resides. At the end of the 21 days, I had connected to a peace within myself that went beyond the pain of my past. My new-found love for myself gave me an even stronger desire to help others. I knew that if I could overcome my pain and suffering, anyone could.

Before leaving South East Asia, I headed to Cambodia to volunteer at an orphanage for children with HIV, Down syndrome and Cerebral Palsy. While there for two weeks, I formed a deep bond with a seven-year-old boy named Heng. He suffered from Cerebral Palsy that had left him bed ridden. Though we could not communicate, we spoke through our eyes. His smile was contagious, as was his total presence and appreciation of the moment. It was through him that I finally understood the deep sense of love and connection that can be achieved, beyond the barriers of language, labels, and judgment. By the end of my time there, I am not sure who was helped more from our friendship, Heng or myself. I still think of him often and believe that he was an Angel in my life.

When I arrived back home to Canada after my journey, I struggled with integrating my new-found inner peace with the fast pace and busy life of the West. I began acting, and though the allure of a flashy Hollywood lifestyle was tempting, I felt a sense of emptiness within me. Deep down inside I knew that acting was not my path to ultimate fulfillment and inner peace – helping others was. With that, I once again gave up everything in faith. I stopped acting and put my focus into how I could help others. It was then that I met Filip, a traveler and photographer from Stockholm, Sweden. We were introduced when he rented a photography studio where I was living at the time. He had a massive heart and an even bigger dream of working with kids around the world. It didn't take long for us to realize that together we could make a difference. Within months, I had packed up all that I owned, left Canada and embarked on a journey of a lifetime.

A few months later, we founded ABC Charity, the first ever human alphabet made with thousands of kids from around the world. In each country we visit, we throw a big event for 500 children and have them form a different letter of the alphabet. Once all letters are complete, they will be sold and JOHN for example would buy J.O.H.N and 100% of the money goes to the charity of his choice. The main objective is to create inspiring and empowering events for children while raising money for charity. Through ABC Charity, we are encouraging children to live a more caring lifestyle and show that helping others can be fun. Despite all odds, Filip and I have made events for thousands of kids in Africa, Europe, the Caribbean, and Southeast Asia and have brought over 1000 children from townships to the beaches and dunes for the first time in South Africa, Namibia and the Dominican Republic.

Though I am still involved with ABC Charity, I have decided that it is time for me to share my story. I hope that in some way I can play a role in helping others overcome adversity, so that they too can transform their pain to power.

Biography:

Ashley Cooper is a Canadian artist, writer, and motivational speaker. Her mission to overcome and transform suffering has taken her on years of incredible journeys around the world. She is the author of #*Pain to Power* and the founder of "The six-step method from suffering to self-realization". Ashley has been featured in hundreds of media outlets worldwide for ABC Charity, which is endorsed by Nobel Prize winner Archbishop Desmond Tutu.

Contact Information:
hello@ashely-cooper.com
www.ashley-cooper.com

Chapter 6
Myth Of Extraordinary

By Nina Hilario

Once upon a time, there was an era of my life that I affectionately referred to as "The Music Video." My manifestation skills became quite powerful, and into my life I attracted extraordinary people, world-class adventures, and luxuries of all kinds. My business was doing well, and I had the love of my life and plenty of friends. Before I knew it, I was living in a southern California beach house, driving my dream car (a white Porsche Panamera with white wheels), and flying in private planes to Lakers' games at a moment's notice. This era of my life was packed with extraordinary happenings. I would be in Bali one week, and at the Grammys the next. The scenes changed so quickly it was like being in my own music video. I lived in Italy, swam with wild dolphins in the Bahamas, and took helicopter rides over Fiji and New Zealand. The music was playing loudly, and I was laughing even louder. I had the experience of finally having everything I could ever wish for. I was living ridiculously beyond my wildest dreams!

Rewind to the childhood years. I came from immigrant parents and a town so poor it was the first city in California to go bankrupt. The notoriety of our town, Vallejo, was ironically kindred because of the fame it gave us. In school there was a twisted sense of pride and celebration when our homicide rate reached higher than that of Oakland, California. Drug dealers and rappers were fascinating because they lived a bigger life. They were the ones who could make something out of the nothing that they came from. In my family and social network, I didn't know of anyone higher than middle class, unlike the fantasy world that was going on in movies and magazines.

In school, we took an early bus into a nicer school district. The kids there had parents who were doctors and lawyers and could afford things that I could only dream about. I went to school wearing cheap clothing (unless Mom maxed out the Macy's department store credit card) and didn't have enough money for lunch or extracurricular activities. I remember how badly I wanted to participate in the Japanese foreign exchange program, and my best friend got to do it while I missed out. Sports, ballet, tap dance, and band seemed like what the other kids were doing who had parents who could afford it, and it sent a painful message to me that I was always trying to hide — that something was wrong with me. I was becoming aware that there were haves and have-nots and that "life was happening for everyone else, but not for me."

Growing up, it seemed my family life was in a constant state of crisis and mental illness. Mom and Dad were doing their best with what they had, but they were always yelling at each other and at us. The pervasive belief was that we didn't have enough money for anything. The situation would get so bad I often couldn't ask for what I wanted without a verbal eruption happening. With issues from gambling, bankruptcy, and physical violence, it was a mad house. Furniture would get thrown, dishes would break, and the yelling went on for long periods of time before there was silence. Seeing kids with a less volatile home life, I felt embarrassed, and I didn't know how to deal with it, so I kept my nose in the books and got good grades. When it was too exasperating I often bolted out of the house with keys in my hand and tears pouring out of my eyes.

I knew there was a happier and healthier way to live, and I was determined to find that better way.

I studied hard and got straight A's. I paved and paid my way through college, eventually graduating with honorable distinction. After college was when I felt like my life really began. I started an endeavor in spiritual studies at a massage school which I considered a "Pandora's Box," you think you're there to learn massage, but the more you study, the more you realize that there is so much more to learn that you never even knew about before! It was fascinating! A never-ending rabbit hole of metaphysical training. I was learning about "energy," and we were required to practice Eastern moving meditations like Tai Qi and Qi Gong. I was realizing the connection between the body, mind, and spirit. I learned how "awareness creates change" and how what we focus on grows. With each class, I took on these philosophies and began to awaken the healer within myself.

Eventually, I began studying the keys to manifestation. My roommate and I had "The Secret" and "What the Bleep Do We Know?" playing on the televisions non-stop. We read books by Deepak Chopra and Eckhart Tolle and the *4-hour Workweek,* and we were determined to live a life of big-time success.

Little by little, the vision boards we made, these little poster boards with cut up magazine pictures made into a collage of our dreams, started working. I would look at my best friend's and mine a year later and gasp. Almost everything on the board was accomplished! She was traveling the world doing acupuncture on a cruise ship, and I had completed my first yoga teacher training in Bali and had taught my first classes downtown.

I realized that our thoughts become things, and the things I focused on were being attracted into my life. As a student, I was working as a free-spirited coffee girl while I was transforming into a creative business woman. I had big dreams and wanted my business to be a successful empire. I began contracting my therapist friends to get massage work at hotels and special events. We had an elite reputation for our "excellence of skill and elegance of spirit," and very soon my clients were among icons and celebrities. I was working non-stop, traveling non-stop, and dreaming bigger and bigger.

With so much momentum in my favor, it felt like I really could have it all. When I spoke to investors, it was like jewels and flower petals fell out of my mouth, and I was negotiating contracts bigger than anything I had ever imagined. This girl was on fire! Everything I touched was turning to gold. It was like having the keys to life, and I had just started the engine, vroom vroom!

I was having so much fun during this era, achieving so many of my dreams, but despite all the success, I found it reached a point where more success was NOT going to be good or better for me. I needed to slow down. I needed to let go of the pressure I was putting on myself to be more and have "just a little" more, but there was no stopping me. I was possessed by achievement, and I wanted to see what would happen if I just had just a little more and a little more… and a little more.

I reached a point where I realized I actually could not have more of anything in the physical world to be happy. I was being gratified but never satisfied. In the beginning, my dream was for freedom, but slowly, as my lifestyle had bigger demands, the dream began to enslave me. My friends thought I was "living the dream," but how is it a dream if it creates enslavement? Sure, I was having fun, but it wasn't sustainable. The pressure to maintain my own status quo and the excess responsibilities made it difficult to keep my life in balance. I manifested great things on the outside, but inside, my joy was being suffocated.

My life had gone too far away from normal, and I didn't know how to let go of this big bubble I was living in without it just bursting. Personal assistants, personal shoppers, a stylist, and a Porsche concierge, it was getting ridiculous. I halfway wondered how much of all this was simply to amuse myself in the movie I was creating?

At my wits' ends, I left for a spiritual meditation retreat in Ojai, California, that brought me back down to earth. I went twenty-eight days into a home with no salt, sugar, meat, outside contact, phone, internet, or money. You had to follow a strict schedule, or you would be asked to leave. At this retreat I began questioning my thoughts and started seeing a new reality. In my mind, I was kicking and screaming until a few weeks in, when I started to surrender. On the weekends I was volunteering at the library and carving out the nature pathway at the nearby meditation mountain. I prepared my own meals, budgeted, and measured, and at the same time each day I sat at the table for thirty minutes eating my meal slowly while listening to classical music. Each day, my mind had less and less spinning thoughts. I got clearer and clearer, lighter and lighter. I saw how I had made up all this conflict by believing I needed to be like someone else or have the approval and acceptance of someone else. By questioning these beliefs, I started to find my freedom. My "okayness." I shifted my perception on so many grievances I once had toward others. These grievances were replaced with miracles. By finding the simple truth, my motivations changed. I was no longer dreaming by a mind possessed with ego. I went from high in the sky, flying from one dream to the next, to being balanced, with both feet on the ground.

Eventually I downsized my elaborate lifestyle. I moved out of the beach house and sold my dream car. Then I took off to Thailand for several months to just BE. I talked with strangers and made friends from around the world, walking through street markets, dancing to local live music, and adventuring into far away foreign villages. When I arrived back in the US, I didn't want to re-create the same fantasy life bubble. So I turned off Facebook, filled my schedule with spiritual studies, and opened up a small, personalized boutique of hypno-healing and coaching practice. I became regular with things that helped me feel connected to compassion and love, like a local Unity Church and Kundalini Yoga.

On my road to inner peace, I found the joy in being an ordinary girl. I didn't need to live an elaborate lifestyle any more or say yes to invitations just because they were exotic and cool. Lucky for me, I had already experienced those things and could see them more clearly for what they were. I politely declined the seduction in my ear to "earn more money" with someone else's dream, trips around the world, or to be married in a mansion or partying in Beverly Hills with celebrities. I said no to relationships that weren't truly or deeply fulfilling. I walked away with love, and I kept walking toward my higher dream. The ego had its hay day during the "music video" era of my life, and I still hear its whispers of empty and short-lived promises to gratify me every day, re-telling the old stories that I'm not good enough or that I would be better if I had something else outside of myself. Honoring myself with my higher commitment toward a daily practice of compassion and a life of LASTING love, I have effectively eliminated so much of this unnecessary pressure and unhappiness. I started to feel normal again; I felt more energy for the things that brought meaning to my life, like warm-hearted connections and helping others to see a way out of their suffering.

One day after a few months of dedicated simple living, one of the guys in a meditation class I was taking gently said to me out of the blue…

"Have you seen yourself lately? I invite you to take a look at yourself."

Remembering what he said, I went home and looked in the mirror. Tears came to my eyes. I wasn't wearing makeup or anything in style. I was not doing anything extra ambitious or special with my life. Heck, I even had fewer friends than ever before, but I noticed my eyes, and they were filled with a light that I could feel in my heart. What I saw was the real me. Pure and true.

You don't *have to be* extraordinary, beautiful, rich, or popular to be at peace in life and deeply satisfied. You don't have to be seduced by someone else's dream. Stay tuned into your own heart. Go at your own pace, and with grace, the nectar of your simple, dedicated, loving actions will be delivered to you. There is a myth that we need to be extraordinary to be loved. I call its bluff! What I have learned from this journey is that when I live simply, it polishes my heart. Without the seduction to be more and have more, I realize the fruit of my labors is having meaningful connections with others, and a sparkling heart from a life well lived, with sincerity and care. And *that* is EXTRAORDINARY!

Biography:

Nina Hilario is a Personal Freedom Advisor and fun-spirited designer of life. People go to her when they want to dream big and wild or for when they want to get out of pain and go deeper into the understanding of relationships, life, and love.

She believes everyone on this earth has a special mission to heal, contribute, and celebrate. Her passion is to share with other people, no matter their struggle, the beautiful possibilities of life via compassionate and consistent cognitive-behavioral therapy, meditational inquiry, and maintaining a spiritual or heartfelt practice.

Contact Information:
www.freedomcoachingnow.com

Chapter 7
Be Beautiful

By Saba Tekle

The winter of 2005 was going to be the start of what I thought was going to be the best year of my life. I had just moved from Seattle, Washington to Atlanta, Georgia to pursue my dreams of modeling. Atlanta was becoming all that I expected it to be and more. I was having the time of my life, and I was meeting all the right people to get my dreams off the ground. The only issue I was having was getting settled. Eventually I found a fly apartment in a prime location, but a week after moving in I received a call from my sister in February of 2006 stating that I should return home immediately, something had happened to Dad.

I sensed there was more to what she wanted to say over the phone, so I pleaded with her to tell me everything. Before she could say another word, I silently prayed, *please God, let him be okay,* she then reluctantly replied, "He died from a heart attack and stroke."

I couldn't believe it. For a moment I thought I was going to be okay. I had just read a spiritual book about life after death. I felt that maybe God was preparing me, but the thought and feeling was short-lived, and I began to break down. I felt the deepest sadness come over me, and I just cried. I cried everywhere: in the car, at the airport, on the plane, until I realized there were not enough tissues for my tears. When I was finally able to embrace my family, it began all over again until my head hurt.

A few days had passed by and I began to notice that for some apparent reason something seemed off. Some family members and friends weren't coming to visit us or weren't calling. When we went to our community church to mourn together, some people weren't sitting next to us. It was almost like the room was divided.

It came to me why, but nothing could prepare me for the reasons or what we faced after. I found out soon enough that they blamed us for my father's death.

A year prior, my parents divorced after twenty-five years of a chaotic marriage. As far as I can remember I've listened to my father verbally abuse my mother. Many, many nights, I would wake up because of yelling and I would get up to quietly listen with my ears pierced against their bedroom, fearing that it would escalate. Every year there was an episode which would end in the police being called or a big divorce scare. Every time this happened my emotions were yanked around like they were on puppet strings because I was Daddy's little girl. My parents separating meant that I wouldn't see him regularly, but when I turned twenty-one, I was over it. I had experienced all I could take.

That year my mother was left with no choice but to file for divorce, and I stood by her side because he began accusing of her of things I witnessed firsthand that she didn't do. Things began to get hostile to the point where we couldn't return home or to our place of business, my family restaurant, Saba Ethiopian Cuisine. My mother had to get a lawyer involved so we could return back to our normal life. That upset my father so much that he began spreading rumors that she had left him homeless and broke. It was fabricated, but most of his family and most of our community believed it, so when he passed they thought it was because of what we had done to him.

I could go on and on about how my father was on Monday through Sunday medications, some of which required not to mix with alcohol, but he still drank Monday through Sunday, or how he suffered from high blood pressure and yet still found a way to get mad at anything. I could also go on and on about how he owned another business that earned him a residual income without him working. But in life, some people don't want to look at facts. Part of his family and community treated us like we didn't have a soul because they didn't know the truth about why my mother had to do what she did. Some didn't even care to find out.

We experienced a whirlwind of events that would make anyone see this world we live in as ugly. Money that was collected on our behalf by the people in our community was kept from us, as well as his car and other things he also had. After the funeral in Seattle, there was going to be an official burial in our home country of Ethiopia, but we were talked out of going for safety reasons. Then when his brothers, my uncles, returned, they filed a lawsuit claiming we weren't his kids.

The crazy thing was, during the last year of my father's life I thought we were fine. I was deeply disappointed, and yes, I sided with my mother, but I expressed that to him. I never hated him. We still talked but not quite as often as he may have liked, and I am sure that broke his heart, but nothing I could say would have changed him, and that was something I had to learn to live with. I also now had to live with the fact that I didn't get to spend much time with him during his last year or didn't get to tell him how much I love him. I wasn't expecting to be judged by others because of it, and I wasn't prepared to face so much of the past pain. I just wanted to remember the father I loved after his passing.

My father was a lot of things, but victim wasn't one of them. He was fearless, intimating, tough, strong, and crazy like most Ethiopian fathers. My dad could beat up your dad. But he was also present, as much as he could be, and loving. My fondest memories of him were when he would say to me, "Do, you know how much I love you?" He would say that like there was a limit to love, and he loved me that much more.

Even his last and only call before his passing was to us because we were a family, no matter what.

I took this pain back with me to Atlanta. The anger, the shock, and the disappointment turned into anxiety attacks. I tried going back to my life of dream-chasing and partying to escape the pains. Sometimes sporadically, mostly when drunk, I'd cry my eyes out or start getting angry at someone for no reason.

It took some years for me to see how lost I was, how much pain I was in, and how asleep I was walking through life. No matter how much I was accomplishing, I had been featured in music videos, photo-shoots, worked behind the scenes, hung out with top celebs, and even been at exclusive parties, there was still this nagging emptiness and ugliness I always felt.

But I had several turning points to wake me up. I remember one day when I was at a gas station. I walked in and paid $20 for pump one, but when I walked out, I realized it was on pump three. I went right back in to tell the clerk. She was an Ethiopian girl, with dark hair and beautiful skin. I thought she was going to be nice, but no, she replied with an attitude. "I put your money on pump eleven, and he already pumped his gas and left. You have to take that up with him."

At that moment all I could see was red. The anger that bubbled up in me was starting to boil, and I had to figure out how I was going to release it. I had purchased an orange juice the same time I did the gas, and the next thing I knew, I was throwing it at her head. I stood there in shock of what I had just done but stood there ready to fight her if necessary. After a few minutes the manager got word of what happened and he replaced my gas, but she still called the police, and I ended up going to jail. This was the second time I had been booked for two hours in a holding cell for something fight-related.

I was released from the holding cell with me having to reflect on all that had transpired. Looking back, I realized I was angry about life — how ugly it was and how ugly people can be.

It took years of soul searching, listening to audio programs, talking to spiritual counselors, and reading self-help and spiritual books, before I could even begin to heal or understand all the emotional outbursts I was experiencing.

The first thing I began to understand was that the nagging emptiness I was feeling was my internal guidance system telling me I was not following my purpose in life. I had learned that I had grown too accustomed to listening to the outer voices, society, and friends, than I was listening to myself, my inner voice. My emotions were drowning out my true self, and deep down what I wanted to do was help others.

Later as I continued my journey within, I learned about the power of my emotions, that emotions are energy in motion (energy + motion = emotion). How they can lay dormant in your system for years, and if you don't release it healthily, you will find a way to suppress it with drugs or alcohol and/or express it at the wrong time and place.

I took this knowledge and I began to use methods like EFT (Emotional Freedom Technique) and meditation with Tibetan gongs. I took these methods and mixed them with some spiritual teachings like acceptance and forgiveness, and that was when I began to heal like never before. During this process I had to learn how to accept and forgive people that were not sorry, to continue to free myself of the anger that was eating me alive. I had to learn to love myself more than to hate others because I had seen what it was doing to my life.

When the emotional clouds began to clear, it was easy for me to see things like I had never seen them before.

I began to see the same community and parts of my dad's family that had turned against us during his passing as people who thought they were doing what was right. I saw most of them as people who loved him enough to fight for him. I saw the others who misjudged us for whatever reason with compassion, because hurt people, hurt people.

The result of my inner work was peace and fulfillment. I felt a peace that was beyond understanding, a peace that felt like how a Buddhist monk might feel or even Buddha himself. It felt natural to feel this beautiful and peaceful and I realized all my negative emotions like anger clouded it, like it did my judgments. Changing my negative behaviors became very easy after that. I also now had a new found energy and passion to pursue my true purpose, helping others heal and find their passion and purpose.

From my experience, if you continue to see the ugly in people, you will begin to see it in life, everywhere, and it will slowly eat at your spirit. But if you give people what they won't give you, love, understanding, and forgiveness, it will feed your soul, and then you will begin to see them through your soul, your soul sees them as beautiful human beings, even as flawed they are, as you are. Yes, you are not perfect; nor am I or anyone in this world, but we are all beautiful underneath it all.

So go heal now, it will release the emotions that are weighing you down, keeping you from being all you are meant to be, beautiful.

Biography:

Saba Tekle is a best-selling author, mentor, and keynote speaker. She was featured in Matt Morris's, *The Art and Science of Success Volume 4 & 7*, and her e-Book *Are You Lost?-A D.I.V.A's Guide To Peace, Passion & Purpose* is available on Kindle. She has a BA in metaphysics, experienced in NLP (Neuro-Linguistic programming), and EFT (Emotional Freedom Technique).

Contact Information:
info@sabatekle.com
www.sabatekle.com
www.facebook.com/sabateklegiorgis
www.twitter.com/sabatekle
#bebeautiful

Chapter 8
Everyone Dies But Not Everyone Lives

By Quandra Adams

"Most people have done all they're going to do in life." They raise a family, make a living, and then they die! ~Les Brown

Take a few minutes to digest the quote above and ponder its meaning in relation to your life. Whew! It puts things into perspective, right? I've heard plenty of times that "we only live once", to "enjoy life while we can", and to "stop and smell the roses", but I have never heard it put quite like this. Nor has anything ever incited a sense of urgency for living life on my terms like this statement, but it's true! Where is the excitement, appeal, thrill, the passion? See, just "making a living" is a problem, and ironically enough, it doesn't allow you to *really live* does it? My favorite college professor put it this way, "There're three kinds of people: the *'haves'*, *'have nots'*, and those that *'have to.'*" Like most people, I was a part of the *"have to"* crowd. I had to get up every day, clock in at a job that didn't afford me the lifestyle I wanted, clocked out tired and grumpy with no time left in the day to do anything for myself other than go to bed, and repeat *yesterday* all over again tomorrow. Since I *had to,* I was a wage slave who was owned by my job and was told when to come, when to go, the amount of money I was worth, and when I would get paid. I figured out quickly that I was merely surviving and not living.

Why would anyone purposely choose to live life like this? For the most part we don't, not consciously anyway. More often than not, we are living from the preset instructions that were given to us from birth from our parents, siblings, religion, peers, the media, authority figures etc. We are not born with attitudes one way or another about money; we were instructed and more or less conditioned about how to deal with money. Thus, our conditioning leads to our thoughts, which lead to our feelings, which persuade our actions that ultimately lead to our results. Take for instance religion as a source of conditioning. My personal beliefs of prosperity started out non-supportive as I was partially raised by a devout Christian, my grandmother, who believed money was the root of all evil. At one point, I was convinced that anyone who had a lot of money was evil, worshiped the devil, and did some unethical things to get it.

My parents, bless their hearts, and black culture probably did me the greatest disservice. My parents' words and behavior taught me that you had to work extremely hard for money and that I would have to do work I didn't enjoy in order to pay my bills. They never hesitated to tell me that, "It's just the way life is." Culturally, it was deeply imbedded in me that traditional education is the only path to wealth. This comes as no surprise to me considering the history of African Americans in relation to slavery where learning was forbidden, thus I was told I had no choice other than to go to school and get a "good" education so I could get a "good" job. So, that's just what I did in the name of following the rules and expecting to get the reward of financial freedom, not financial bondage. In fact, my first degree must not have been "good" enough because I went back and got my masters. After graduating, I had an epiphany that I want to share with you. Stop the paper chasing. Not just the money, but most importantly, the other piece of paper: the degrees. After racking up about $120,000 of debt between two of my degrees, it finally hit me: this is not how to build wealth. Seriously, why am I taking out $100,000 worth of student loan debt with interest to make a $35,000 salary that is going to be taxed? I'm not saying there's anything wrong with learning. I'm saying you need to know without a shadow of a doubt that you have a burning desire and passion for your chosen career path, and you know what the projected starting salary is. Most people are drifting aimlessly through life hopping from job to job because they never took time to really think about what their passions are and how to live from them. This will always cost you time, energy, and money. We go to school because we were told we had to or that it's the automatic path to wealth and at some point this may have been true, but not so much now. Today job security is an obsolete thought since we cannot be sure that our companies will be around long or if our positions will be outsourced. I learned that if I am going to thrive I must possess a skilled trade, have a product and/or a service that solves a problem, or be an expert in a field.

My first financial goal was to save $10,000 in 10 months. I knew this would not be an easy task especially considering I was making less than $26,000 a year. When I reached that goal, I decided I wanted to coach others on the mindset and the method that made this possible for me because I learned how empowering pursuing financial freedom can be. As you now know, I didn't start off with a prosperity mindset. So in order to start saving money the first thing I had to do was recondition my thinking by replacing the old thought that I would be associated with evil and greed if I accumulated money. Second, I had to learn the foundation of budgeting, which is to spend less than you earn, always pay yourself first, and always have an emergency fund. Third, I had to take action and have confidence that I would achieve my goal. I began to track my expenses and reduced or eliminated anything that was not a necessity. I separated my accounts, and I put everything on auto draft. Once I put the system in place, to ensure I would reach my goal all I had to do was remain consistent because at that point saving $10,000 was only a matter of time.

Turning my passion into a business required me to replace destructive thoughts as well. Remember, I had been raised to believe that in order to pay my bills I would have to do work I didn't enjoy. This created a disconnect for me because I developed a passion for empowering people and I enjoy doing it so I gave myself permission to pursue my business. This time I decided that I would make my own choices and not consult my preset instructions that would have told me I couldn't do it. In order to make my business a reality, the first step I had to take was to proceed in spite of my fears. The fear of failure and the fear of the unknown can be debilitating when starting a business. More often than not, it's these two fears that keep people from ever pursuing their dreams. Second, I continually invest in my business and financial education by attending seminars, reading books and collaborating with business owners in my industry. Lastly, I knew in order for me to be successful I needed to hire a mentor. I knew this would allow me to gain knowledge from someone that had been where I was and is where I want to be. I made this decision because I understand a mentor can save me time and energy by identifying all the obstacles I would face and inform me on the best ways to maneuver around any challenges.

Even though I had not been told the truth about money, I figured it out. As long as you are doing what you love, you'll never be working hard. Imagine the possibilities for your life if you had complete control of your time and worked when you wanted to, but doing only what you love and for which you have a passion. How much more could you accomplish not only for yourself, but for your family and the world? We are here to express ourselves in the most fulfilling way possible that will bring joy to everyone in the world, and you cannot do this from a place of *"have to"*. It has to come from a place that allows you the freedom to create, without inhibition, in order for you to tap into who you really are. There are gifts and talents inside of you right now, bestowed upon you from the most high, and when you use them, it is an outward expression of God's love inside of you for others to enjoy and be inspired by. Don't believe me? Think about your favorite poet, singer, speaker, writer, or anyone that has ever left you in amazement. When these people are doing what they love, they are operating in a God-like state of being … they are in the Zone. The place where one experiences peak potential and all performance seems effortless. Again, you cannot operate in the Zone from a place of *"have to"* because there is little to no love or passion in the space of *"have to"*.

I encourage you to identify, examine, and dismantle any conditioning belief that is keeping you from living life on your terms. Now that you are aware of the role that your conditioning plays in your decision-making, you can consciously choose to let go of any beliefs that do not support you in your quest for wealth, and you can replace them with beliefs that are supportive. Please understand every thought you have about yourself in relation to money is either helping you or hurting you. Let's face it, you are going to believe something so why not make your thoughts serve you.

Biography:

Quandra Adams is a Motivational Speaker and Abundance Coach. She has always been an inspiration to those in her inner circle, and now she is sharing her gifts with the world. She is unsurpassed at breaking down money matters in a humorous yet logical way that will cause you to experience a paradigm shift in your thinking. She holds a Bachelor's in Political Science and a Master's in Business Administration, but the messages she shares comes from the prestigious school of Hard Knocks. Join the legion of smart women at www.quandraadams.com who are consciously creating their financial futures by receiving the weekly newsletter that covers current debt elimination strategies, tips on getting out of the rat race, how to uncover and monetize your passion and MUCH MORE!

Contact Information:
www.facebook.com/quandraadamsabundancecoach
www.twitter.com/quandraadams
info@quandraadams.com

Chapter 9
My Financial Love Life

By Michelle Fox

It is 1:30 in the morning and I...cannot...sleep. Visions of the judge asking me if I'm sure that I don't want alimony clouds my head. Slam. Thoughts about which credit card has enough credit left to put gas in the car and food on the table tomorrow. Switch. Memories of beach vacations and an unavoidable aching fear that I won't be able to revisit that lifestyle. Boom.

This is just one example of the many sleepless nights that have occurred after my divorce. Leaving my husband was one of the most liberating and terrifying experiences of my life. After being together for twelve years, our relationship became stagnant, and we began to live like roommates for most of the second half. I believed that there had to be more to life than what I was living, but it also felt financially safe to be tethered to a man who had an excellent relationship with money (attracting it, saving it, investing it, etc.) I found the courage to leave in order to find my own path.

I left the marriage with a resolute decision to begin a fresh start at creating a life that felt joyous and authentic. I was growing resentful in our relationship, and I felt extremely weighed down by my circumstances.

I moved in to a studio apartment immediately following our separation. My goal was to minimize my spending while I transitioned out of a joint financial relationship. My intention and my behavior turned out to be drastically different.

I created over $25,000 in credit card debt during the two years following my divorce. This was horribly embarrassing. I became depressed thinking about my debt. I felt trapped in my current lifestyle, and I felt too ashamed to share my secret with friends, or anyone in my family.

It hit me like tidal waves once I realized that I had to pay off this huge debt on my own. I was slow to see how I created the debt so quickly, and it took time to come to terms with my spending behavior. Operating on my single income was quite challenging after twelve years of sharing household expenses and enjoying two incomes.

In my desperation, I thought about asking my former spouse for alimony as he typically averaged about twice my salary through his real estate pursuits. At the time of our divorce, I denied any monthly alimony payment as I believed it would keep me emotionally tied to him. I was clear that I wanted a complete separation and independence from the relationship. After years of living in a mediocre marriage in an effort to remain financially safe, I was ready to prove that I did not need to depend on a partner for my financial well-being.

I remember our first home purchase as a married couple three years into our relationship. It was thrilling to move out of our cramped two-bedroom condo in the city and into a three-bedroom Denver Square in a park community. The home hadn't been updated in at least thirty years, so we had our work cut out for us.

We redesigned the entire residence, bringing in fresh walls, a gourmet kitchen, an updated wood fire place, a Jacuzzi tub... I loved that home. I loved that we created something together. I loved that we now had space to host parties and entertain guests from out of town. I believed that we were happiest as a couple during this joint effort to create a home and a place to build our family.

Our connected goals translated into financial abundance relatively quickly. My realtor husband increased home sales exponentially for the next three years. I also had a comfortable income to contribute to the household. We enjoyed the financial freedom to take a beach vacation at least twice a year in addition to the traveling we did to visit extended family. A new dog named Maya was welcomed into our family circle. We never had a budget, and we just kept a rule that we'd check in with each other for any purchases over $250. We had a bi-weekly home cleaning service, and we both drove luxury cars. Life was very comfortable.

Some friends of ours, who also happened to be neighbors, decided to move to an upscale neighborhood and into a mini-mansion. It was always a treat to have dinner at their new home, mainly because of their company but also because it felt like I was visiting another world, a world that you normally have to be wealthy to visit. It never occurred to me that it might be my reality a year later.

Because of my husband's connections, he was able to find a beautiful home in that upscale neighborhood at a discounted price. He convinced me that moving to this house would be a profitable investment in our future. He painted a beautiful picture about hosting even larger parties and even more out of town guests with the added bedrooms and bathrooms. He also pointed out how great all of the schools in the neighborhood would be. This, of course, pulled on my heartstrings, as I so desperately wanted to have a baby.

My heart sank a little bit with every conversation we held about a move. As I mentioned before, I loved the house that we were in. I went into the renovation process with a vision of building our family in that home.

I eventually submitted to his desire to move with cautious optimism. It turns out that it felt great to entertain and show off our wealth. It was also a nice treat to have access to outdoor pools, multiple walking trails, and a great dog park. We ended up adopting a second dog named Jazz in this house. Many beautiful memories were created there.

Due to the increase in mortgage (about double the payment as our previous mortgage), our twice a year vacations went down to one. Our shopping sprees quickly ended. Our trust in each other's spending habits eroded. We were living for the house as opposed to having a house that supported our desired lifestyle.

Moving to the mini-mansion in the upscale neighborhood was the beginning of the demise of our marriage. Sure, the new house was a dream home, but it never felt like it was mine. It felt a lot closer to a museum than a residence.

I did not listen to my intuition when it was screaming, "Don't chase after the American dream; chase after YOUR dreams." I take full responsibility for contributing to the choices we made.

I would love to tell you that my experience with the houses immediately re-aligned me with my values. I cannot. While it was a part of my process, I wasn't conscious of my decisions for four more years. In that time, we downsized our home, adopted a beautiful little girl, and divorced soon after.

My experience of overreaching financially in my marriage and overspending post-divorce has pushed me to examine what I truly value. What I have learned is that I value quality time with friends and with my family. I value financial freedom. I also value contributing conscious work to the world.

I no longer have the luxury of a house cleaner, multiple vacations, or lavish dinner parties. What I do have is financial awareness, more confidence in my financial future, and a certain optimism that my daughter will benefit from the lessons I have learned.

My financial belief has always been that if I work hard, then I deserve to play hard. I have been humbled since my divorce as I realize that yes, I enjoy working, but there has to be a balance between what I bring in and where I am allocating my money. There needs to be space for savings, an emergency fund, and retirement plans. I am happy to report that I am currently contributing to all three and am confidently on track to reaching my goals.

I created a spreadsheet from the previous year that helped me categorize all of my spending. It helped me to see EXACTLY where every dollar had been spent over the last year. This allowed me to find that I could give myself a $1200/month increase in cash flow just by cutting out careless spending on things like drive-thru lattes, monthly spa treatments, and a housekeeper.

The really fun part is that my spreadsheet showed me how I can be completely out of debt in less than three years. I have called this document My Financial Love Life! Notice I am avoiding the word "budget", which sends me into an emotional frenzy.

I chose to write down my negotiable expenses (Netflix, spa treatments, coffee house visits, etc.). Next to each of these expenses I wrote down my alternative choice to save money (Redbox, self-care, coffee at home, etc.). Looking at this list every morning reminded me that I had control over my choices and over my money. This eventually translated into more self-confidence and more self-trust.

I committed to no longer use my credit cards, and I applied my newfound overage to my higher rate cards first. I also committed to tithing 10 percent of every paycheck to a place that nurtured my spirit as well as committed 10 percent of every paycheck to my personal savings account. My employer contributes to my retirement fund. I am two years in to my plan, and my debt has been cut in half, my income has increased, and my savings and retirement have steadily grown.

I am committed to My Financial Love Life, as it is a means to have more peace in my life. I am in love with the idea of living debt-free. I am in love with my capability to make it happen.

When I feel that my financial house is in order, it is easier for me to be present with my daughter and with the people I interact with on a day-to-day basis. It has also been a means to create restful sleep.

Biography:

Michelle Fox is an intuitive healer, psychologist, and divorcee. She is the author of the forthcoming book entitled *The Graceful Divorce*, an intuitive guide through transition. Michelle received her degree in Applied Psychology from New York University. She also received her post-graduate certificates from The Inner Connection Institute (Clairvoyance and Channeling) in Denver, The Arvigo Institute (Spiritual Healing through plant medicine), in San Ignacio, Belize, and from Sonia Choquette's Practitioner Training Level 2 (Six Sensory and Intuition) in Chicago. She was born in Boston and raised in Denver, where she currently resides with her daughter.

Contact Information:
www.michellefox.com

Chapter 10

Freedom – Live the Life You Always Wanted

By Vanessa Cunningham

"I believe that one defines oneself by reinvention. To not be like your parents. To not be like your friends. To be yourself. To cut yourself out of stone".
—Henry Rollins

As a young child, you are innocent, with no worries in the world. At most, you are worried about playing with Barbie dolls or playing in the park, going ice-skating, eating ice cream, and the list goes on. Unhappy feelings are foreign to you unless you are crying for something that you want and your parents don't give it to you. As you grow older you may start experiencing different feelings and/or emotions, which may seem foreign to you. They can be feelings of isolation, loneliness, and even low self-esteem. But where did they come from? You may wonder, why do I feel this way? The next thing you may wonder is, "Who can I turn to?" When those questions go unanswered, then what happens?

I remember being a very outgoing child. I loved to laugh, smile, sing (mostly yelling), and enjoyed participating in school activities. But that came to an instant halt at the age of ten. I'm now entering the fourth grade, but this time I'm feeling less confident. My body looks different; I put on a couple pounds. I no longer "looked like everyone else." I didn't get teased at school, luckily for me. It came from the people that I expected to guard and protect me, my family. The word "fatty" become something I now heard on a daily basis. This is the first time I had experienced feeling a sense of isolation. Being shy became my new norm. I had no clue of what to do. I began to notice myself dimming my light. That bright and vivacious kid now became hardened. I was angry, defensive, withdrawn and bitter. I kept a lot of things to myself. On the outside I may have appeared to be fine, but deep down inside, I was hurting.

I can say that I had what appeared to others as a great childhood. My mom and dad were great providers for me and my siblings. I went on great vacations, I generally got what I asked for, but I still always felt emptiness inside. I didn't feel "safe" to express my feelings. I had a tight family in that we looked out for each other, but I wouldn't say we were emotional or expressive of our feelings. In fact we rarely said, "I love you," no one talked about his or her issues. We just did our own thing. So, I did just that and handled it the best I could, by pretending all was well. This was the start of what I like to call the "daily inner battle.

When I would attend family functions, like barbeques, those feelings were exacerbated. Now I was experiencing public scrutiny that made me always feel like all eyes were on me. I was always asked, "Oh, what do you have on your plate?" Meanwhile, no one else was being asked. I would always brush it off with a snarky comment, but deep down inside, I was hurt. These instances didn't allow me to feel like I could just let myself just be. I was constantly reminded of the area I fell short in my life – my health. My hardened heart transpired into an attitude of: "Nothing bothers me" and "I got this, don't need your help." Often times I misconstrued situations as a direct personal attack to me because I became highly sensitive. A part of me just died.

This became very evident in the earlier parts of high school. I remember focusing on the last thing that really mattered, which was being cool. I made sure I became friends with all the upperclassman. I barely did any schoolwork, although I managed to get decent grades. I was very critical of who I hung out with, often times judging people based on how they looked and not their heart. This would be the first key to unlocking the start of my quest to find what I was good at. I took initiative to try and discover what excelled at.

Midway through high school I got a wake-up call, which I believed was from God, and I started to slowly change my ways. I had to think of my future, like how the heck would I get into college? I began to do work and study, which I realized came very easily to me. In fact, I picked up haters VERY quickly. The ones who did well, that were probably secretly judging me, began to wonder: *How could someone go from barely doing anything to receiving A's on everything?* That one switch enabled me to feel alive for the first time. I began to seek out what I wanted for myself. I started to be an active player in my life. In fact, I went against what everyone else was doing.

I took on business and computer classes, which I ended up loving. I began my quest to dig deeper into what I wanted to do. These shifts gave me the confidence to tackle my weight issues. I lost thirty pounds and went from a size 12 to a size 6. After graduating high school I went off to college with a better outlook on life. During college, I got myself involved with many organizations and even became a part of a sorority, Alpha Kappa Alpha Sorority, Incorporated. What I noticed throughout those experiences was that, with everything I was involved in, I still had those same struggles, which ultimately manifested in wanting to feel apart. To those around me they never saw me as someone who struggled internally, but I did what I did best, I acted like everything was okay. It became apparent that there really was no personal growth in how I wanted to really feel, and in how I treated others. The major shift for the worst took place when I entered corporate America.

Now I was in a competitive environment (which I didn't think would be an issue as I'm competitive by nature), but I now had to work closely with folks of varying personalities, office politics, and criticism on work performance. Those feelings of "Am I good enough?" and "What do people think of me?" quickly resurfaced in a major way. I often found myself again in constant conflict with myself. There were very specific moments, like when it came time to doing presentations, which I was required to do quite often. Those moments were grueling for me. I was constantly stressed out and often sick. Then I also noticed the pounds piling on again. What was strange to me was that although I had a desire to be a great speaker, I often ran from it. My fears would either make me make up excuses on why it should be postponed, or I would do it last minute. Last minute practicing meant I wasn't confident, as I would constantly question if I gave it my all. This resulted in a vicious cycle of self-torment. What I noticed during those times was that the old lies I used to tell myself just kept resurfacing, and that what I used to tell myself wasn't true. And because I never allowed myself to talk about how I felt inside, it would just continue to manifest in different ways. It took a long time for me to accept my greatness and to know that I had earned every great thing that happened in my life.

Your situation may look different than mine. For me, it was being overweight as a child and allowing the projection of others to torment me. For you, it may be different, but the struggles may be the same.

I wish I knew how to fully enjoy my life. So many years of my life were not enjoyable due to the torment that I would bring on myself. I'm in a better place today because I did the following things: I invested in a personal development coach, on a daily basis I quote scriptures from the bible, I read positive affirmations, and I also share my story. These actions have been instrumental in my healing process.

Today I can thankfully say that I'm operating in purpose and passion. I always knew deep down inside that God was preparing me for something bigger than I could imagine. That prompted me to save up for my exit (whenever that time presented itself) and I also enrolled in nutrition school. Even though I excelled in my corporate career, I was extremely unhappy. I reached a point where I could barely get out of the bed in the morning. I debated for a year and decided to take the leap of faith and leave corporate America to start my own company, Unhealthy No More. I teach busy professional women to thrive at work and in life by creating nutrition and wellness plans specific to their lifestyle. I also emphasize that healthy living isn't all about fitness and eating healthy, but also about nurturing the mind and making time for spiritual practice.

I'm writing for major publications, speaking at corporations, and I'm helping people live their best lives, which I enjoy. I now take the time to celebrate my accomplishments and myself. I'm bold enough to declare what I want and go after it. I now believe in myself, and my abilities to be the bold, confident, and courageous woman God destined for me. A constant reminder for me is, "God hath not given me the spirit of fear, but of love and of power and of a sound mind." (2 Timothy 1:7).

You have one life to live, be happy, conquer all, fail and get back up, love, and enjoy, because life is short. If you change what you say and think about yourself, the right things will come to you. What you say, you become.

If you have dealt with issues of being overweight that have stopped you from being the best you or have hindered you from pursuing your dreams, or you are carrying around a lot of emotional baggage, I invite you to grab a copy of *10 Ways to Live a Happy and Healthy Life* to help you begin your journey at www.unhealthynomore.com/freegift.

Biography

Vanessa Cunningham is a Huffington Post contributor, nutrition and wellness expert of Unhealthy No More, Inc., author, and speaker based in New York City. A graduate of Pace University, she also studied at the Institute of Integrative Nutrition. She helps busy professional women prioritize their health by creating customized plans that are fun, sustainable, and easily integrated into their hectic lifestyle. Her expert advice can also be seen on Essence.com, MommyNoire, and MindBodyGreen. Her adoring fans have called her a "tell it as it is coach" and a "transformational coach.

Contact Information:
www.unhealthynomore.com

Chapter 11

A Self-Love Journey

By Denita Austin

I believe our childhood has so much to do with who we are as an adult. My story is of the awkward girl who was bullied and teased throughout school. I was lonely because it was so hard to make friends and connect with others. Since I wasn't the most appealing looking kid, no one would be seen with me. This was something that I struggled with constantly. Now, of course, like everyone I knew at the time, I wanted to live in the Huxtable home on the Cosby show. Their family structure was based on values and morals. I was able to relate to so many situations that occurred on that show that I would dream I was in that family. *There is nothing wrong with dreaming right?* Dealing with so many emotions and just being confused about connecting with others caused me to isolate myself from other people. My self-esteem wasn't the best, and depression settled in at a young age.

I was the tall skinny girl with glasses and crooked teeth in high school. I was called names such as olive oil, clown feet, lollipop, pencil and tall glass of nothing. I still didn't look like the cool kid that you wanted to hang out with. After school, I made sure that I sat up front near the bus driver so that I would feel safe from being attacked or harassed. That tactic didn't work at all. The kids would throw objects at the front of the bus, trying to hit me with their best shot. The bus driver wasn't able to help simply because she was focused on driving the bus.

I really couldn't focus on my schoolwork or anything relating to school because my mind was preoccupied with what would happen once the bell rang. Thoughts ran through my mind like, *is someone going to be waiting for me after class? Will there be a group of girls waiting to jump me?* I was exhausted with my own thoughts. I didn't know what to do.

Underneath the pain of being bullied, there was a strong urge to prove myself and, honestly, I didn't know to whom I was trying to prove myself. I would try any and every thing to be accepted. I would wear the latest fashions and hairstyles, but it still wasn't enough. I would even walk around without my glasses, knowing I couldn't see a fly on the wall. I was running out of ideas fast, and my self-esteem was getting lower and lower. I dealt with this throughout high school and it didn't get any better. School for me wasn't pleasant at all. In my mind, I felt like the world was against me. I felt like I couldn't trust anyone.

One thing I noticed about everyone who bullied me was that they all appeared confident. They appeared as though they had it together, at least through my eyes anyway. I asked myself over again, *what is it about them that I admire?* The answer came to me … I admired the fact that they were popular and were liked by many, but after giving it some thought, I really admired the seeming confidence that shined so brightly without a word being said.

Being so afraid to stand out and be confident in my own light was always frightening. Because I was made fun of and picked on every single day, I became angry and frustrated. I didn't want to go to school at all. I felt alone, and I experienced a sense of sadness that I couldn't explain. No matter what I tried to do to be confident and make friends, it never worked.

This word "confidence" was a mystery to me. *What is it, and how do I get it?* The word played over and over in my head countless nights. How can I be confident when I don't like one single thing about myself? My heart was screaming aloud for it, but I just didn't have the answers. I was looking for a step-by-step guide. I needed someone to take me by the hand and show me what life was like on the other side – the side full of confidence, self-love, and happiness.

These emotions continued over the years – depression, anxiety, and anger. I wore these emotions on my shoulders at all times, but I wore them with a smile on my face.

I was so relieved when I finished high school. I said to myself, "Yay, no more bullies; I am free." Little did I know, it didn't stop there. As I transitioned out of my teenage years and into my 20s, I noticed that I started to run into the same issue in corporate America. Yes, I said the curse word: Corporate America.

Corporate America was hell in the beginning stages of my jumping out there. I honestly didn't know how to connect with other people because I never could when growing up. So this was a major challenge. I remember asking a few co-workers to hang out but not knowing the proper way to do so. I also tried to hold basic conversations not relating to work to get a feel of comfort and maybe hoping that we had something in common. I was actually still an outcast in the work arena, oddly enough. Women would have huddles of conversations about me loud enough for me to hear them, just to ruffle my feathers. I would never be invited to anything, or included, for that matter. That made it super awkward at work. I would get mean stare downs for no reason at all. I remember on several occasions being told that I would never amount to anything because I was simply not like them.

Deep within my heart and soul, all I ever wanted were friends that actually loved and cared for one another. I was looking for something sacred and valuable. Now, as an adult, *how do you find valuable friends?* Trust me; I didn't have the answers at all. In my mind, I figured as women, we all share some of the same issues and obstacles. I figured that I couldn't be the only person desiring this. Just because we are considered adults doesn't mean we automatically have it together. The same friendship, love, and support that is needed as a child, doesn't change as an adult. Why not talk about them and connect with one another? I felt like we could only help each other grow, right? Well guess what, not everyone thinks or feels that way.

It took years for me to really understand that in order for me to have confidence or friends, I must have self-love first. It took me actually being tired of being tired. I was fed up with how I felt. Looking in the mirror and not feeling good about the person I had become due to previous experiences made me even more enraged. I was craving something bigger than myself.

Life can be creative, fun, joyful, vibrant and spontaneous. It can be anything I make it. This is what I continued to tell myself over and over again in order to stay motivated. I told myself that it was okay to be vulnerable and free within yourself. I had to have more courage for some, simply because it was scary out there.

I went through a trial and error phase of self-love many times because I could never stay on track. One month I would have it together, happy and full of life, extremely social with others and appearing confident with who I was. Then randomly I would fall into a slump with mental and verbal abuse to myself. This would go on and on for months.

Going through this trial and error phase repeatedly caused me to really evaluate my life and how I was making decisions and handling situations. Apparently, something needed to change and it was definitely my way of thinking. If something isn't happening in life naturally, I learned, do not force it. Forcing only makes it worse. This experience taught me that not only is forcing the worst thing ever but being resistant to change falls in the same category. I had to make a decision to step outside the box – and my head, for that matter – to try a different approach at life and for myself. If something isn't working for you, it's time to try a different system.

It was not until I jumped into the 30s arena, when a light bulb went off, and I felt like enough was enough. I noticed that time was passing me by and the decisions that were made previously really didn't get me very far. I was in quicksand and didn't even realize it. I wanted more and I knew that I was the only person that could change my life around. I was the only person who could make me happy and create the life that I wanted. I also knew that in order for me to have the friends that I wanted, I had to make that happen too. Most of us don't like to admit it, but we actually need one another in so many ways and on so many levels.

The person that I needed to guide me on a self-love journey did not exist for whatever reason. That step-by-step guide or book didn't exist either, or maybe it did and I needed someone to expose me to it. I figure that if I created one for myself and went through the steps, that I could share my experience with other women on their journey. I wanted to create something that would help women looking for that guidance.

So, my self-love recovery compiled into a daily regimen filled with meditation, yoga, a healthy diet, reaching out, and a lot of soul searching. I had to make a commitment to myself that I am loved and worthy of it. I began focusing on things that made me happy. I switched up a few things in my life to get different results. These were drastic changes that were needed in order to grow, but I found my step-by-step:

- **Spend Time Alone**

Being alone doesn't have to be a bad thing. When I spent time alone, I was able to see a different side to my personality. I learned more about myself mentally and emotionally. I was also able to focus on parts of my personality that needed improvement.

- **Daily Activities**

Find something that will feed your soul and help you begin your day on a positive note. For me, it's all about the meditation and yoga in the morning. I'm able to clear my mind and begin my day with a fresh start. This is also my alone time. Meditation reduces my stress and creates a space to make better decisions. For you it may be running, biking or long walks. Make this a priority simply because this will be the first thing you do to start your day.

- **Diet**

By all means, I am not a diet expert but I do know what foods work for me and which ones don't. Instead of eating food that will leave you feeling tired and drained, choose something for your palate that will increase your energy and make you feel alive. This is super important. It's not always about taking care of yourself on the outside. Work your way from the inside out. The results will blow your mind.

- **Own My Individuality**

I stopped apologizing for who I was. I no longer shied away from my gifts and talents. It wasn't important to fit in any longer. I realized that I was beautiful, amazing, and phenomenal on my own.

- **Build Courage**

I stepped into my own truth of truly being myself. Not being afraid to just be me and do the things that actually made me happy. I noticed that my energy and vibration changed. I felt motivated and empowered to keep going in the direction that my heart said to follow.

- **Build Your Belief System**

I started believing in myself and my abilities. The goal was to beat fear so that I could believe in myself. Create affirmations or a mantra of your choice to recite. This was a daily practice of trying something different every day and thinking outside the box to push through the negative thoughts. It takes time to get to this place, but once I got there, any goal began to seem possible.

- **Explore and Discover**

Now this is the fun part! I took the time to explore and discover what feeds my soul. I made it about what inspired me and moved me in life. This is where I celebrated me, **just because.** When I took time to do the things that I loved, delicate smiles were placed on my face from pure joy from within, and guess what? I was responsible for that!

You too can follow these steps and you will be amazed at the outcomes. Consistency is the key to begin seeing the results from your courage and hard work.

My results were impeccable. I was eating better, my skin cleared up from not being so depressed and stressed and I was getting the best sleep ever. I was able to step out in the world not being afraid to be me. I felt responsible and enlightened because of my daily regimen. I became active and I had more energy to do things throughout my day. I learned to take time out for myself, and my thoughts, for that matter. I felt alive and it was easier to surround myself with the same energy from others. Most importantly, I loved me and after experiencing all of those things and staying committed to myself, I was able to step into leadership and move forward in life without being afraid.

So here I am today, a woman who is exposing her soul and essence of vulnerability. I speak about the importance of self-love on my radio show, *The Hidden Cove*, every Sunday. I connect with women all over the world to share, motivate, and empower others. I now believe we are here on earth to learn, love, grow, inspire, motivate, share, and create.

I encourage you to find your circle of supporters on your journey of self-love; it makes the path easier to follow. These beautiful spirits do exist, and they enjoy shining and seeing you shine as well. Build your foundation based on love, honesty, integrity, and respect. It will make life so much easier.

Biography:

Denita Austin – Mentor, Author, Yoga Coach, Artist and Visionary Leader – is dedicated to traveling the world as a philanthropist and entrepreneur. She strives to help us connect and understand our co-operative responsibilities as a global village. After practicing and teaching yoga for over 10 years, it is now time to connect with others on a deeper level to explore the possibilities of something bigger yet to unfold.

Denita is known for her passionate and creative self-expression of support and love for others. Her energy and vibrant spirit is inspiring and warm hearted. Her journey continues to unfold as she spreads love in the world one heartbeat at a time.

Contact Information:
www.DenitaAustin.com

Chapter 12
Queen
By Lisa Campbell

I was brought up in a family that surrounded me with love. I was raised to respect others, work hard, and have a plan for my life. My plan was to go school, to get a good job, and get married so I could live a decent life. But I wasn't told much of what life or love consisted of until I experienced life for myself. I guess there was only so much my parents could tell me.

Growing up, the people who I hung around were much older than I was. So I was going to the hottest clubs, bars, and strip clubs, even dating guys that were older than me, most of which consisted of drug dealers, NFL players, and a few well-known local guys. What most people started doing around 18 or 21, I was doing at the age of 16. Also, at an early age I had a source of income; I had a job throughout the time I was in school. I even moved out and got my own place during that time. I was able to manage balancing work, school, and partying.

One night I met this guy at an event. He was a charmer, attractive, had money, and was established. He began to spoil me with attention, affection, and lavish gifts. He knew the rights things to say, the rights things to do, and the right things to buy me.

I started to give up partying and drinking to give this guy a chance because he was so persistent in pursuing me. What can I say? The first year was amazing! I fell for him hard, but the second year was when the craziness started.

When I would go out with my friends, it would be an issue. If my friends would come over, he would have a problem with that too. He would say...

"Why do you want to go out with those girls?"

"If you go out with them, don't ever talk to me again."

"You're friends are going to try to break us up."

"I know when you're around them you talk to other guys, and eventually you're going to want to leave me."

I knew he was just paranoid, but in my defense, I'd reply, "Because they're my friends, and I hadn't seen them in a while."

Eventually I gave in. I was young, naive and vulnerable, looking for love through a man. I thought he just loved me that much, and that's why he was so jealous. Slowly I stopped hanging out with my friends. So we were together all the time after work and school.

Then things took a turn for the worse. It was a friend's birthday party, and since I hadn't been out for a very long time, I figured he wouldn't mind if I went. So I told him I was going out, but it didn't take long for him to get mad. He began accusing me of trying to cheat on him. The argument escalated, and the next thing I knew, I was on the floor. He had hit me in the head.

I was in such a shock that I was speechless. I didn't know if it was the pain or because I couldn't believe what just happened. I just laid there on the floor and allowed him to continue to yell at me. I figured that if he let it all out, then he would calm down.

Once I got up from the floor tears started to roll down my face. I forced myself to call my friends and told them I couldn't make the party because I was sick. Once he heard that I had cancelled, he embraced me and told me he was sorry for hitting me and that he would never do it again.

The next day at work I received a lot of roses and jewelry, including earrings, a ring, and bracelets. That was his way of apologizing to me. Then he assured me it wouldn't happen again, so I kept it to myself, because I believed him.

Slowly my sister noticed a change in me, I stopped calling her and going to see her like I used to. She knew something was wrong, but I would insist that everything was okay. She had met him a few times, but for some reason I never introduced him to my immediate family.

My family gathering was coming up.We would get together every so often to spend time together. I was excited about seeing my family because I felt confined and isolated in our relationship, so I told him that my family was having this event and that I would be attending it. I was left with no choice but to invite him because he was getting angry.

He refused my offer and began an argument. The argument quickly escalated, and next thing you know, he hit me *again.* But this time it was so hard I went unconscious. I woke up to see one of my friends, an ambulance, and some police officers. I just blanked out as they put me in the ambulance.

I remember the tears rolling down my face and the blood running out of my nose. I found out from my doctor that my nose was fractured, my lip was also busted, and I had two black eyes.

My family was called and they came up to the hospital to see me. They asked me what happened, and I finally told them everything while feeling so ashamed.

My family embraced me as I cried in the doctor's room. My dad and uncles were enraged, and they wanted to hurt him. Other family members began to pray; they asked God to cover and protect me. They began to encourage me by saying that I'm a beautiful queen and how no man is supposed to put their hands on me.

It all began to click, and I needed to make some decisions, quick. I moved out of my place and went back home. I changed all of my contact numbers. I feared for my life, so I quit my job after a coworker of mine informed me of all these gifts that were being delivered. Lucky for me, he didn't know where my parents lived, but unfortunately he knew were a friend of mine lived, so he would pop up at her house to try to relay messages to me.

At this point I knew he had some serious anger issues and problems that were above and beyond my reach, because I knew his anger towards me wasn't from insecurities. Come to find out, not even a year later he had been locked up for murdering a guy!

But at that time, to get through it, I began to start reading my Bible and realized that I almost allowed somebody to steal my joy, my worth, my freedom and the position that God had given me at birth, a queen.

A queen is defined as a woman who inherits her divine position at birth. The more I read and prayed, I started to gain my birthright position as the strong powerful woman that God had seen me as all along.

I'm sharing my truth to encourage all to know how beautiful God made us. We are all powerful queens!

It can be hard to believe, and the journey might be long, but if you do these three things, you can heal from whatever may get in your way:

- Love yourself
- Be true to yourself
- Love God

Don't ever be afraid to leave a bad situation or change; if you thought it, do it. Fear is not of God and we can conquer over it! When you're able to turn your negative situation into a positive one, you've learned the true meaning of transformation, and you turn your story into God's glory.

Biography:

Lisa Campbell is currently a PhD candidate in General Psychology and has an MBA in Business Administration. She is an author, motivational speaker, lover of God, and certified life coach. She is passionate and dedicated to inspiring anyone that's willing to work towards their purpose.

Contact Information:
Orleathia.Campbell@gmail.com

Chapter 13
The Climb Of My Life

By Liz Nead

It was the final week before my twins' high school graduation, and in the midst of recognition nights and graduation parties and commencement, I was preparing to climb Mt. Kilimanjaro in Tanzania. I worked out for hours each day, preparing for the 19,000-foot trek to the ceiling of Africa. I have to confess I was not looking forward to another band concert, as I slid my sore 40-something body into the unforgiving plastic seats lining the musty auditorium. Yet, this was a poignant moment: their final activity as high school students and mine as their constant witness.

As the melodic notes of *Hosts of Freedom* swirled around me, I saw a different kind of mountain below me. I realized I had just completed something more challenging and trying than attempting to summit Mt. Kilimanjaro. This final band concert marked the conclusion of the climb of my life, from despair and rebellion, to renewed vision and purpose.

The ascent began 18 years ago in the deepest of valleys of inauthenticity and struggle. Desperately trying to manage a life that constantly threatened to spin out of control, I volunteered to coach a girls' track team at the local Catholic high school after quitting my own track career in the middle of another disappointing season. Only a few years older than them, I chased my lost potential during our warm-up runs, in their lilting laughter and excited self-exploration. I was about to launch into my own unknown; it had been three months since I last had my period, and, while I had never missed a cycle, I rationalized it away with fierce denial.

When I could no longer explain away the swelling in my breasts and abdomen, I confessed to the coach. He firmly and swiftly released me. Mother Mary looked accusingly at me from every corner of the school in her various forms, maintaining her position as the singularly revered pregnant mother among a group of Catholic schoolgirls. I walked away in shame, thankful the hot flush couldn't be detected beneath my brown cheeks. I had betrayed my lineage, my history. The Virgin Mary was not the only saint turning over in her grave. I came from royalty, East Indian Christian royalty.

The Original Vision:

I am the oldest daughter of my parents' American dream, a love story that winds through the south of India among the waving banana plants and burgeoning cashew trees of Kerala. My family was converted to Christianity in Syria, by the "doubting" disciple of Jesus. Drawn by the promise of eternal life, they gratefully followed the saint on his spiritual mission from Syria to the southern part of India. They dubbed themselves "Marthomites". They were not an official part of the spiritual and social ladder of Indian caste system, but they slowly adopted Indian customs, submerged in ritual, constant festivals, and elaborate costumes until the God that brought them to the endless green hills was almost forgotten. Great-grandfather would embrace the spiritual basics of the Brethren denomination and strip away the flamboyant gold-threaded sari dresses, replacing them with wraps of white purity.

My father was the beneficiary of this dream when he chose, at age 14, to make his fortune in the United States of America. Over fifty years ago, while attending college in the bustling southern Indian city of Mumbai and preaching at a local church, he found his love. She was a nursing student. I'm sure he was taken with her bright intelligence that still shines through flashing amber eyes and her carefully scripted properness. He boldly lived his vision, replacing her Indian name with an American moniker for an American wife: Alice.

He asked "Alice" to follow him to America, painting his destiny as if it were already written. They lived apart for more than five years, only corresponding in writing. He enclosed an envelope and postage with each of his letters, asking her to stand on the roof of the nursing school and face America as she read his elegant looping handwriting.

As I rubbed my hand over my belly, pregnant with truth and shame, at the time, I had no knowledge of their sacrifices for the American Dream. They didn't try to inspire me with their wedding, gifted to them by a small church in Detroit. I didn't hear of the Jewish driving instructor my father hired so his bride would know how to drive. Behind the scenes were long hours of driving between Detroit and Minneapolis after Dad was accepted to the University of Minnesota doctoral program. He never shared what provoked him to remove himself from the program with only a few credits to spare. I can only imagine the excitement my mother – a girl who carried water skins made of goat bladders – must have felt picking out wall to wall shag carpeting and matching paint for her new house in America.

Their legacy to me would be First Generation vision, a gift of sure success for the daughter of immigrants. Their hope and plan was that I would not have to suffer or labor to achieve my dreams. I could enjoy my place among the citizens with my flat Minnesota accent. They wished for me an idyllic suburban existence, which would begin with college and end with an overflowing retirement plan. Sacrifices were no longer needed. In fact, they were no longer appreciated. I need not risk at all when they had carefully budgeted peanut butter and jelly lunches every day, saving every penny to ensure my success.

Their sacrificial desire to secure my success produced the opposite effect. I only felt the burden in this ill-fitting immigrant's vision, chafing and choking my freedom to "just be American." I crafted my own First Generation vision, a drive to escape the burden of imposed and pre-defined success. All around me were forbidden fruits, peach-colored boys with icy blue eyes and drunken excursions in pursuit of popularity and a full social calendar. I began creating the pattern of my own visionary messes. Striving to break free, I careened forward into another disaster I couldn't explain.

It all came to a head in this pregnant moment. My twin sons developed, my belly ballooning forward until everyone knew my secret: I was the prodigal daughter who was completely unfamiliar with my true self and unworthy of the genetic gifts and advantages I had inherited.

For 25 years, my parents tried to grind out my rebellion with silent cold stares and thrashing discipline from a newspaper-wrapped stick from the cherry tree in the front yard. I wanted to experience the tantalizing fruits that existed beyond that backyard. They only wanted to keep me from the over-sexualized and crude American culture threatening to invade and destroy their dreams for me.

Yet, in nine months, my mutinous vision had given way to another. In the final days of a waning relationship with a hometown boy, two new lives began. I called my sister with the pre-marital news. "Please tell Dad for me. I can't face him." It only took a few minutes before the phone rang and I had to face my father's disappointment as he once and for all released his original dreams for me. Everything changed in a moment. Juicy late-night boyfriend conversations over last minute homework were replaced by half-off diaper deals at Walmart and the cold sterile realities of the obstetrics office. I hung on to the remnants of my parents' white picket fence as I rushed through the raging currents of my new life: convincing him to marry me, a C-section, a shotgun wedding. All for my two coffee-colored sons who came arrived just weeks before Christmas, their skin lightened with a touch of America. Just enough to look like the highest caste of the Indian system to which my family never belonged.

The Suburban Vision:

With the same passion with which I pursued the hazy pleasure of belly-baring provocative skirts and leering college boys, I now carefully and resolutely constructed the safest life for my Indian princes, marked by manicured lawns and PTA meetings. It was an ode to all I thought my parents envisioned. Together we pretended not to see the results of my Chinese water torture marriage: his inability to see my virtues, my increasingly dark temper. I refused to let got of my dream of a perfect and redeemed life while I released the twins' father, claiming I had found the love of my life. I blithely moved into this second marriage with broken spirits and impossible expectations. Each morning I stared in the mirror and a crazy stranger stared back. Extend the lashes, cover the circles and straighten the hair: no one would see my inner chaos as I drove to recapture my father's imagination and my own potential.

The one-bedroom rental gave way to a five-bedroom house I couldn't afford. To pay for the house, I stuffed my exuberant personality in the bottom drawer of my grey-walled cubicle and dutifully climbed each rung of a ladder in the financial corporate world. Insecure and miserable, I donned my motherhood each day, signing up to be a homeroom mother, making soups from scratch, and purchasing as many Legos and Matchbox cars as my bank account would allow.

Our house was the cornerstone of my picket-fence vision, an unremarkable structure blending into rows of boxes lining the suburban streets. It represented my ability to receive my birthright – success I could provide for my sons at any cost. I hung on to this talisman through any circumstance, refinancing with a variable interest rate loan, borrowing money from friends I barely knew, begging for help from family members who knew my story all too well, and fighting with my husband when he wanted to flee this ark of self-destruction I had created.

The truth came to me a different way in this vision, through the "mortgage man," waiting to give me a slip of paper – 90 days to respond or I would lose my white-picket monument to normality. I didn't answer the constant requests to pay my eight months late mortgage payment, afraid to hear a voice that reflected the self-loathing woman who could no longer afford her life. I hid, breathing shallowly as he banged on the door to my tattered vision. It was at this moment I allowed myself to see my reality, and I let go. My silly, hysterical suburban vision floated away into the mid-western sky. Finally, I allowed my lungs to be filled with a deep breath of ancestral wisdom from hundreds of years before; I reluctantly opened the door and received his message.

In the end, I had to leave it all behind, thankfully choosing to protect my children, my marriage, and my sanity by moving to a rented house just down the road. Redemption seemed impossible, so I sat in the full truth of my own disillusionment, pretending to succeed at my work and trying to repair my marriage. It would be on another path that my vision pushed forward. It started as a nagging feeling that I was meant for something more than this, but the entanglements were too great. How could I claim my purpose without upsetting the carefully balanced mess that was my life? As I walked past the shelves of books claiming to teach financial balance and marital bliss, I picked up a book, and an odd thought popped up, "If I am ever a speaker, I need to know what's out there." *Wait. What?*

The brain is an intimate cave, filled with all the dreams and hopes from generations passed. One rebellious and then obedient *First Generation Indian Princess* could not alter it. Coursing through my blood, the followers of St. Thomas – sandal-clad and wrapped in white – clasped brown hands together in prayer for me. The burgeoning legacy of my grandfather burst open, and in that moment, I knew. I wanted to stand on stage, as a speaker. I would inspire. I would tireless share my story of disillusionment and redemption until we all became the children of the pioneers of clarity and purity.

The Inspired Vision:

With poster board and photos and phrases I cut out from *O Magazine* encouraging me (to Live My Best Life!), I created my first "vision board." I affixed everything I ever wanted to that small square of impossibility I hung behind my bedroom door. I was too old to host a television pilot, designed to inspire. I didn't even know anyone in the radio business, how was I to get a radio show five days a week? I lived in the middle of the country, in a "fly-over" state. How would anyone find me to speak on stage? But each morning, as I stared into my board, my true self, with all the possibilities of generations of hope and vision, stared back at me. Over the course of weeks and days, the dam of self-doubt and guilt broke apart, allowing for a series of happenstances. A conversation with a television producer. A proposal to a program manager at the radio station. A friend needed a speaker for their professional women's group. As I opened my heart and allowed everyone to see my purpose, – my hope, my need to serve – the answers flowed in. Once I released my purpose to run free, stopped living for others, relinquished the need to punish myself for not doing better, and opened the door to just do better, those dreams became visions and those visions became my life.

A month after my sons' final band concert, I would climb the 40 miles to stand atop the mighty Kilimanjaro, lungs pinched with the oxygen-deprived air and heart full of African love and mystique. But before I experienced the clear transformational atmosphere of the summit, I stand atop another mountain, in a high school auditorium at a band concert. *This* climb began with an uncertain phone call to my father, "Dad, I'm pregnant." I summit today watching the twins on stage in their final high school activity, one playing the French horn and the other the euphonium. As the notes drift away, I release my sons to find the joy in chasing their purpose, to fail and wipe the sweat from their brow, only to dig in again. To never give up and stand on the foundation of hundreds of lifetimes lived by the forebears of these fortunate two. I too will robe myself with something amazing – hope for the future and the pursuit of my purpose.

After the concert, the twins received scholarships for college. One was for harmony, bringing people together. The other was for leadership. It looks like the legacy has continued as it begins anew in them. Liz successfully summited Mt. Kilimanjaro on July 4, 2014.

Biography:

Liz Nead is a television host, speaker, life and business coach, and author. She has been featured in several national magazines, including *Ladies Home Journal*. Her television show *Life Dare* has been nominated for a regional Emmy and won an Iowa Motion Picture award. The mother of seven children, Liz is married to a retired military officer. She continues to pursue her vision to inspire others with her life, which most recently involved climbing Mt. Kilimanjaro and raising money for several charities.

Contact Information:
liz@neadinspiration.com
www.neadinspiration.com

Chapter 14
Broken, Bitter, & Bankrupt

By Sharonda Lynn

I'd be lying if I said that I came from a broken home. I would also be lying if I said that I never had the blessing of feeling loved, being supported, pushed, and having someone to trust when trusting within myself was not good enough.

The truth being, no matter what background you emerge from, you are not exempt from the lessons God has for you. Sometimes the lesson feels as if life is attempting to destroy you, but it is not until later in life when you discover that it was all meant to help you grow and build character.

Sometimes when I sit and reflect I can feel the same intensity of emotions that I felt on that very morning. I often wonder, if I could go back and reverse time, would I? Or would I entrust in the road that God placed me upon for his own personal reasons? I can still hear my father knock on my door in a state of panic. I could feel the intensity in the air, and my gut feeling told me that something was wrong. "Your mother needs you right now", my father said. The tone of his voice was filled with worry.

I will never be able to forget what I walked into.

My mother, the mother that had always been so strong and unbreakable, was gasping for air and uncontrollably spitting up white fluid. Seeing my mother like this took me to a place where no thoughts existed, just simply stillness and disbelief. I had always been taught that the best answer one can seek comes from God. So I immediately started to pray. Within the midst of my prayer I heard my mother's attempts to speak. I could hear the struggle and the pain of her trying to gain enough wind within her lungs to say something. Somewhere in between gasps my mother said... "Ronnie I love you, take care of your father." Her eyes rolled to the back of her head, I hugged her tightly as I prayed what felt like the world's longest prayer, and she collapsed in my arms. The paramedics rushed in and pushed me to the side in attempt to resuscitate her. All I was then left holding onto were my prayers.

I was once what many would refer to as a track star. At several different times during my adolescent years I was the fastest girl in the country and my mother was my biggest fan. She exemplified what being a strong black woman was and represented. She was an influential parent, foster parent, and dedicated social worker.

The passing of my mother left an emptiness, one in which I convinced myself could be filled along the way. I was broken, when you lose a part of you that is so deeply embedded within the person you are, you never return to whom you once were. No one but those closest to me noticed these changes in me.

My world changed and things that were once passions were now pressures. Running track and being a scholar athlete was once what I took great pride in being. Yet everything had become mundane, the excitement that I once held for track and my passion for school was now nonexistent. In result, I replaced my faith for my flesh, my faith was weakened, and it was failing me. My flesh hadn't failed me, or at least that's what my belief was. Until I woke up and realized my late night lusting that I used to replace the emptiness had transpired into an unwanted pregnancy and morning sickness.

Fast-Forward.

I am in Detroit, secretly eight months pregnant by my ex-boyfriend. I felt ashamed and bitter at the choices I myself had decided to make.

On November 6, 2001, around 10 o'clock at night I started having sharp pains in my stomach. Once I reached the point that I could no longer endure the pain, I had no other recourse but to reveal to my dad what had been held secret from everybody for so long. Without any questions my father rushed me to the hospital. The next day around 11 o'clock in the morning I gave birth to a healthy baby girl.

My father was very supportive during this process. He looked into my eyes and said with the most comforting voice, "Ronnie, you could've told me, you did not have to go through this alone." All I could do was cry, through my sobs I told my father, "I never wanted to disappoint you."

This was supposed to be a time of celebration, but that was far from true. This was a time of grieving, in all actuality there was a part of me that knew that I had already lost her. I was only seventeen years old, I was nowhere near ready to be a mother. So I did what I thought was necessary. I put her up for adoption.

During the adoption process, although I was physically present, I was emotionally absent. Everything was going so fast. I didn't know how to feel. One thing that I did know, it was too late to turn to back now. When asked by the few that did know, I created my own truth, I simply said she died, because either way I had lost her, *Right?*

This part of my life, or the events that had taken place stayed between my father and me. By now the emotional ramifications of my decisions had taken away all I had saved within my emotional bank and I was now heading toward the line of bankruptcy. Still, offers of full ride scholarships to top universities for track were rolling in, but I had no desire to accept them. Track hadn't meant the same to me without my mother. So eventually, I just moved back to Seattle, got my GED and a fake ID. During this time my father had become my lifeline, and I in many ways his. I had developed an ongoing battle with fear, fear of losing the last person that truly loved me unconditionally.

To balance all of my lows, I decided to get high, and my drug of choice became men and partying. Disposable men, disposable pregnancies, and disposable friends was the way of life for me. I never put any effort in relationships of any kind because I always knew there would be an expiration date. I had no feelings.

I wasn't ready for love but sometimes love has a way of sneaking up on you. So, I embraced it, and in return this was the distraction I needed, wanted, and yearned for. Robert was a very close friend since we were teenagers. He was the shoulder to cry on in times of pain., but who would guess that he'd be the cause of many of those tears within my future?

I sacrificed my happiness for his. I loved him more than I loved myself. We were inseparable. I admired his drive. I observed his dedication and it pushed me to pursue my goals and take my passions beyond merely thoughts. By this time I was in school for social and human services (inspired by my mom) and working at a non-profit. He was-overseas playing basketball, living out his dreams.

I was broken, so becoming co-dependent was an easy outcome. I believe my codependency was the beginning of our destruction. Usually, when a woman exhibits jealous or possessive behavior it stems from the insecurity of losing him to the hands of another woman, but in my case it was the fear of losing him to the hands of the one above us.

The true test to anyone's character is not how many tests in life you are faced with, but how you respond to those tests, and to overcome them. This next phase of my life will by far be the hardest test I would ever have to overcome.

They say when someone passes away a new life is born. At this time Robert and I were expecting. I was four months pregnant when I received a call on May 29th, 2009 at 6 o'clock in the morning that my Father had passed away. The words spoken not only penetrated my eardrums but also my body, causing it to hit the ground. Nothing made sense, my Father was in a rehabilitation facility recovering from a knee replacement surgery. I had lost my father, my best friend, and my hero all within a split second. Once again what was supposed to be the happiest time of my life was void of anything even resembling that emotion. I would be lying if I told you that I was not angry with God, because I was. Who would ever guess that I would have to learn to forgive God for taking the two people who gave me life away?

Five months later I gave birth to what saved me, my healthy 10 pound baby boy. I then vowed from that moment on that whatever I did would solely be about him. I wanted him to experience the love that my parents had given me while they were living.

The next two years were long and I was still grieving. I was raising a son and dealing with a distant and cheating boyfriend. What was privately going on between us began to become public. Cheating was common but more so in the shadows. It went from women overseas, to women from down the street, to women that I worked with.

I went through a phase of reflection after. Even if I wanted to give up I couldn't because it was no longer just about me. I now had a second life to also consider, my son's. This phase of reflection brought many things, one of those things being a new love in which I never would have invited in or expected to fall the way in which I did for him. He was my beautiful disaster and my wreckful awakening. He forced me to face myself in a new way, a way of truth and accountability. Prior to him I was running from my past and not wanting to accept the mistakes I made. He made me question my decisions and face who I wasn't facing, myself.

So much can occur within just one split second that can have the propensity to alter the person we become, forever. There is so much that we bury beneath the sand in fear of what others might think of us. I was guilty of this. I still don't know if joy came within the morning, or within the night, but it came. Maybe not easily, but it came. It came through the release of the anger I had held upon so tightly to towards God, and the acceptance in the role I had within my own shortcomings. What also came was the realization of the choices that I made, the ones which set me upon the path of me feeling broken, bitter, and bankrupt. I had to stop making excuses, pointing the finger, and finally become accountable for my actions and behaviors.

I am no longer ashamed of my past indiscretions. I am no longer being held captive by my past. My past made me the woman and mother I am today. What once was me holding onto a prayer, now is me holding onto God.

Biography:

Sharonda Lynn is a proud mother of her four-year-old son, Robert 'Duce' Bishop, and a believer of the power of accountability, who has risen above her circumstances to make a positive impact on her community. She is a dedicated social service professional, serving in a variety of capacities for the last six years, ranging from community advocate-case manager, Life Skills Coordinator, her current role, Sharonda helps run a housing program for young women between the ages of 18 to 24, who are escaping a life of sexual exploitation and trafficking. Sharonda has many interests and is overcoming adversity by being a mentor for young women, by empowering them to recognize their worth, being accountable, and helping them achieve their personal goals.

Contact Information:
iamsharondalynn@gmail.com

Chapter 15
It's All About You

By Samantha Hess

I understand how this title sounds. You are probably thinking, "It's all about you? What kind of advice is that?" You might be thinking, "That sounds very self-centered and narcissistic." Well, it is the best advice I have ever received and the advice I wish I had listened to about one year ago. I'll explain through the story of my biggest life lesson.

On January 31, 2014, I was travelling at a trade show with my boss, who was president of a company in Silicon Valley, and his wife. We were talking about a game he would play in his head when travelling, and out of nowhere we developed an idea for a new social application. That was on a Friday. The following Monday I received a call from him saying he had developed a business plan and was leaving his job as president to pursue this project full time. He also wanted me to join on as co-founder, and by the way, there was a documentary crew that wanted to film the journey as well.

Now this is the thought process that went through my head at the time, "I am twenty-four and have only been working in marketing for two years. I have no previous business experience besides what I did in college. Why would he want me to join him on this crazy journey?" I truly felt inferior and that I was not good enough to actually really contribute to the app. So what did I do? I lied.

I immediately responded, "Of course! Let's do this! I can go in 50/50 with you. Money won't be a problem." I built myself up as this successful 24-year-old who had taken on a business before and could take on one now. I had zero money and zero experience doing anything like this before, but I was the one who took the game my co-founder played in his head and added demographic info to it to create a revenue model. I saw what this could do for my future. I didn't believe I was good enough, so I lied to make myself seem better.

As you can imagine, this all came crashing down quickly. Within a few weeks, I had to tell him I couldn't produce half the funds to get the company going. Then a few weeks later, my entire story was revealed as a lie. All of it was caught on camera for the documentary as well. This was my all-time low. I remember sitting in my room after getting exposed on camera and just thinking about how I was going to feel as I was packing my things and leaving. Where would I go? What would I do? Should I start applying for jobs? Why did I think it was a good idea to lie?

So the next morning I wandered out and waited to be told that I needed to leave immediately. My boss was there, and he asked me to sit down. This is what he said, "Here's the deal. I do not trust you. I do not believe anything you say. You will never lie to me again. I knew you were full of shit the whole time. So now we start fresh, but it will take you a very long time to win back my trust, and if you lose your confidence in business, you are done. I will kick you out and not think twice about it."

This was obviously not what I was expecting, but I wasn't going to argue. I wanted to stay, and I wanted to see this through to the end. So we kept on going. A few weeks later we were driving back from a meeting and I asked him why he didn't make me leave after what I did. He responded, "Because you are very smart. You have great ideas, and you bring a different perspective than anyone here." This was the moment that truly changed my life.

I realized at that moment that I had been good enough all along. I really was an important part of making our app and our documentary a success. I had no reason to lie or portray myself as something I was not. I felt like I lost myself as a person as well. When you are pretending to be something that you are not for so long you start to forget the person you truly are. It is not something you can adjust from quickly. The only reason I was able to move on was because I recognized my faults and embraced the fact that I was still moving on. Now don't get me wrong, it's not like everything was fine and dandy from there on out. I still cringe at what I did every time I think about it, and I will never be able to have the same business relationship with the people I work with again, but I am one of those people that tend to not listen to others and do what I feel is right at the time, and then deal with the consequences later.

So why did I tell this story? Because this experience taught me the most important life lessons I will ever have. Here are my takeaways for you to always remember:

Everyone makes mistakes…and it's OK.

Everyone is human, and we all make decisions based on our emotions at that moment in time. They may not necessarily be the best decisions we could have made, but if we always made the right decision we would never learn or grow as people. I look back on my decisions and how I got up to this point. I am not happy with some of the decisions I've made along this journey, but I wouldn't have it any other way. How we handle our decisions and learn from our mistakes defines how we will progress in the future.

I feel like I lost myself in the process because I was pretending to be something that I was not, when in reality what I really had to offer was more than enough. I only came to terms with it when I accepted my decision and moved forward with the app and the documentary.

You have to be your number one supporter.

It all starts with you. If you walk into a room and are not confident in what you are presenting, then no one else will believe what you are saying. You have to be your number one supporter; otherwise it will show when you don't even realize it yourself. Always remember that everyone has something to offer, even if they are right out of school. Each person brings their own unique perspective to a situation, so deliver your opinions confidently and with authority.

Be bold enough to follow your dreams.

I realize this sounds extremely cliché, but it is very true. Throughout this entire journey I can't even count how many people have called me crazy because I quit my job to pursue an app that has a one in a million shot of actually making it. However, I live my life by the number of regrets I have, and if I didn't choose to do this, regardless of how I got there, I would have regretted it for the rest of my life. So if you have an idea or passion that you want to pursue, don't let reason or logic stop you. Go for it!

And most importantly, never lose yourself.

No matter what obstacles you face on your journey through life, always remember to stay true to who you are and never feel like you have to pretend to be something you aren't. Your qualities make you unique, and your uniqueness is what makes you valuable to whatever project you are working on. When I lost myself and stopped believing in who I was, I sunk miserably and couldn't focus on anything. Only when I got back to being me and handling situations the way I would normally do did I finally come back and gain even more confidence than I had before.

These pieces of advice are why "it's all about you," because it truly is. You are the one who makes things happen in your life, you are the one who brings the confidence and forces others to listen, and you are the one who keeps yourself true to who you are. You are also in control of your own life, and never let anyone take that away from you. So go out there, wear your confidence like armor, and conquer the world one dream at a time. If you stumble or make a bad decision, remember not to sweat it, forgive yourself, be sure you get the lesson, and handle it with courage. If you do these things, no one will be able to stop you! Cheers to all the amazing women out there!

Biography:

Samantha Hess is the co-founder of Salmon Social, a social app that launched in Boise, Idaho, in May 2014. With her partner, she developed and launched the app in 90 days. Her company was granted Boise's Hottest Startup in May 2014. Samantha also founded a production company, Red Coconut Productions, and is producer on the film titled *Crazy Social.* She is an advocate of female entrepreneurs and is featured in The Huffington Post discussing this topic.

Contact Information:
samantha@salmonsocial.com
www.twitter.com/SalmonSami
www.facebook.com/salmonsocial
www.salmonsocial.com

Chapter 16

Be Your Own Love

By Dixie Garcia

It was the summer of 1998. I was eleven years old and playing in our backyard with my brothers and the landlord's daughter, my only friend at that time. After a few hours, my baby brother Jordy wanted to go back into the house to use the bathroom, but he ran back to us to tell us the door was locked. My brother and I were confused. This was unusual because my mother knew we were all outside. What was even odder was that the top and bottom were locked.

I just happened to have the keys so we all ran back to open it. Within moments of the door swinging open we witnessed a sea of blood right at the entry. We screamed for my mother, and she came to us covering her nose with tissue.

My first thought was, *The secret is out.* I knew what had just happened, but my brothers didn't. They were confused and couldn't make sense out of the situation because up until this day, they never knew that my father physically abused our mother. It was something I had kept quiet since the age of six. I hated my father, and I wanted him dead. Now my brothers understood why, but they still loved their seemingly perfect dad.

Growing up, since I was the only girl, I had my own bedroom. When my parents had their problems, my mother would sleep in my bed. I would just pretend to be asleep as she crept in, while boiling in anger, thinking how badly I wanted to keep my mother safe, but how could I? I felt that if I did, he was going to do the same thing to me as he did to my mother.

By the morning she would be gone, leaving traces of blood stains behind, but my brothers never saw her walking out of my room.

As we got older there was less physical abuse, but the verbal was still happening. I was tired of the situation and hated being home. I wanted to live a normal life where I wasn't stepping on anyone. I also wanted my privacy. I was working at Dunkin Donuts, almost forty hours a week so I didn't have to be home, but it didn't help. I was still tired of living with hostility so I decided to "runaway" to my aunt's house. After a heart to heart with my aunt, I decided to go back. The same day I came back I forced my mother to make a decision. I made my mother choose between my father and me. She chose me. By the weekend he had moved out, and to this day, this event hasn't been spoken of.

After four years of peace and living somewhat of a normal life I thought that abuse and drama was all behind me, and like every girl, I wanted to have fun and experience love. I was so innocent and full of dreams. All I knew were the nightmares of my parent's relationship, but I wanted to believe in fairy tales and love at first sight.

It was rare if I went out. My cousins went out often and knew everyone. We lived in a small city where everyone knew everyone, but I didn't. One night out on my cousin's birthday, April 13, 2007, was when I meet Joe. He was five years older than me. He had just finished college and had a job making good money, legit money. We started dating and he swept me off my feet. It was all I knew, so everything he did was amazing, I didn't know any better.

I was warned by my cousin to watch out. I didn't know the club culture and its etiquette. I didn't know at the time that a club might be a second home to these men.

It turned out my man was one of them. He would know when there was fresh meat at the club since he knew everyone. He would have all the background information on the women: if they had kids, a man, and who had been their past partner. So, when Thursday would come around he always had some excuse to not make time for me. There were family events I was never invited to, he was either working late, or had something with his kids.

Not only did I find out that he was a womanizer, I also found out firsthand that he was an abuser. I slowly became my mother without the physical abuse. All the arguments we would have were always turned into how unworthy I was, how my friends weren't good for me, and how I was a bad person for holding onto a grudge towards my parent. He would also always want me to explain to him why I was staying at a dead end job.

All I wanted was time with him.

I kept staying because I had convinced myself that I couldn't find anything better. I saw my friends dealing with the same thing or worse. I spent five years back and forth with this man. The last and final time he broke up with me Joe claimed it was depression. He had lost his job and didn't feel worthy enough to keep around. Even after we broke up, he still tried to come back around.

One day I was talking to my cousin, Shari, about how it was a coincidence right before our breakup that so many guys were trying to get with me. How stupid I was for being so convinced I had the love of my life and saw these guys as a waste of time. That's when she told me about the picture online. It was of Joe with another girl that dated as far back to when we were dating.

How dumb can he be? Of course, my cousin was going to know about this and tell me all about this girl. That same night, I got a text from him at 2 o'clock in the morning. My body was full of rage, all I was thinking was, *Why is this fool still texting me?* So I ignored it until the next morning. It turned out, his house burned down, and he was looking to me for support. My heart dropped to hear this, but the anger came back. I couldn't see or think straight. He still had the nerve to try to manipulate and question me about why I couldn't help him or why I wasn't there for him. He thought I was going to be his ride or die no matter what happened between us. I laugh to this day at how much nerve he had.

I learned then that I didn't know what a healthy relationship looked like besides what I had witnessed. The women I had around me also had convinced themselves that this was life. They would tell me, "You're not the first one to deal with the cheating. What he did to you, the next guy will do the same. So, honey just stay. It will happen anyway, no matter who you were with."

Those words would hurt. I didn't know how to break this toxic cycle, but I decided I wanted to be in a healthy relationship. I've been into self-help and personal development since my freshman year of high school. After years of reading, I made a connection, everything reverted back to self-love. I learned about being your own love before going out looking for a relationship, because no will love you unless you do.

After reading more articles, blog posts, and books, I kept seeing this word "life coach." So I Googled it like I do everything else. It looked like something I wanted to do one day. I decide to be a client first to make sure it was something I wanted to do, and it was a great experience. I learned what kind of coach I wanted to be and I was becoming the person I wanted to be. Because of her, I healed what was left to be healed and found my purpose through it. I got certified, and that was also a fulfilling experience.

I got into coaching now wanting to celebrate women and cry with them, to show women and young girls their true currency, because now I knew my worth, our worth.

I am currently teaching women and girls to be their own love, and that your self-love is the status symbol.

Biography:

Dixie Garcia is a certified life coach, speaker, and teacher. She is the founder of Be Your Own Love, a program focused on empowering women to find their worth and live their purpose with boldness. She is also a student of ACIM (A Course In Miracles). Dixie is currently working on writing a book for young women about being their own love. She's also developing a workshop about Finding and Living Your Purpose with Stephanie Ghoston.

Contact Information:
www.cultivatedsense.com

"Andre, what do you think your true calling is?" - Oprah

"I don't know" – Andre, Oprah's Hairstylist

"Of course you know what your true calling is."

"I don't know can you change callings?"

"It looks like you're a hairdresser; you've done my hair now for 30 years, but no it is not just doing hair. You are about the enhancement of beauty. That is what you do.

You bring an enhancement of beauty."

"People get so messed up about callings they think it something big. They think there has to be some big, "I am called like Moses, the burning bush and God is speaking to me." So now I have to "do" something with my life." – Oprah, *Super Soul Sunday*

Chapter 17
Tears of Purpose

By Zaneta Aycox

I remember like it was yesterday. One hot summer's day I ran into the house and plopped down in front of the bathroom mirror with hot tears running down my face. I looked at the girl in my reflection as if to say, "Help me." Although she cried also, watching her was comfort for me. She always happened to exude a lot more hope than I felt.

It all started with a mane that just couldn't seem to be tamed. I had been teased almost every day for having wild hair. So to recently have my hair braided by a neighbor seemed to be the perfect antidote for my social problem of being taunted and ridiculed. Well, I was wrong. I felt beautiful as ever, whipping my hair braids back and forth. I wished I could make every girl in the world feel this beautiful. Then it hit me — when I grow up I want to be a hairdresser. This became my dream. It wasn't just so people can look beautiful. I was convinced that if I could make people *feel* this beautiful, the world would be a better place. From this moment, I was on a mission to change the world.

On this particular day I sat outside with my friends, each of us going down the line having the "when I grow up" conversation. When it was my turn, I smiled and said proudly, "I want to be a hairdresser when I grow up." Well, I had no idea I would be ridiculed with an outburst of laughter from all of my friends.

"Not with that hair," and, "How are you going to do other people's hair when you can't do your own?" my fellow peers remarked mockingly. Even though my thick, tangled, fuzzy ponytail had been replaced by neat braids, I still couldn't catch a break. I felt like I would be marked for life as the girl with the crazy wild hair. Then I felt it, a lump rising up in my throat. I could barely swallow. I tried to play it off. I jumped up and bolted into the house. Before I could make it up the stairs to the bathroom and lock the door behind me, the tears started flowing. I was hurt. I felt hopeless. I hated that my hair was wild. I hated that my crazy hair became my label. I felt out of place. The words of my family rang over and over in my head, "You have hair like your dad." It sounds as innocent as "Oh, you have eyes like your mother." However, I knew what they were really saying. They were letting me know I had hair that was different from theirs.

With my father being Black and my mother being Puerto Rican, my hair didn't identify me with my mother's side of my family. My hair was very different from the long luxurious waves that my mother was known to have. I felt ugly. I felt like I had inherited a disease that no one could cure. I sat in front of the mirror and just cried. I just wanted people to think I was pretty. I just wanted to make people feel pretty. I just wanted to change the world. That day I decided to do something about it, I looked at myself in the mirror and made a commitment to that 7-year-old girl looking back at me, "I am going to be a hairdresser." Ten years later, at the age of 17, I passed the New Jersey state board exam to be a licensed cosmetologist.

Every client became part of my mission. Every time I had the opportunity to put my hands in a client's hair, I was putting my hands into their world. I began to know their story. I began to know their fears and their hopes, their dreams and their failures. Two hour hair appointments became my two hour platform to make that woman feel courageous and beautiful enough to overcome any insecurity.

I remember anxiously waiting for their next appointment to receive feedback about whatever we dared to believe. While they sat in my chair getting styled, we would discuss different ways to overcome challenges in life. The challenge may have been to find motivation to finish a degree program, ways to better cope with a difficult relationship, or beginning a weight loss regimen. Whatever their concern, I was on a mission to help that client be the best they could be by being proactive in their approach to life. I befriended and became a part of my clients' lives to the point that I received much more satisfaction from seeing their lives transformed than I did them trying out a new hair color. There was the mother that struggled with postpartum depression, the woman whose business venture just failed, the lady who found out her husband had been having an affair, and the student who was trying to balance single parenthood while pursuing a dream — they all became a part of me. Every time I encouraged them, I was also encouraging myself. How can you speak encouragement to someone that challenges them to believe like never before and you yourself do not hear your own words?

Dare to believe was not just born out of my own struggles, despair, and challenges, but every client that I've ever had the pleasure of putting my hands in their world. The proverb still holds true that "as iron sharpens iron, so a man sharpens the countenance of his friend" (Proverbs 27:17). We all have had our share of ups and downs. When we are down, we know how much it means for someone whose faith is a little greater than our own to pour hope into us. Well, we never think of the person that does the pouring. However, they too are strengthening their own self. Iron sharpening iron is a two-way street.

Just like that 7-year old girl in my reflection, she cried just as much as I had. The only difference is I know she had more hope than I. That was all the comfort I needed. She understood me. She knew why I cried. She knew how alone and misunderstood I felt. When everyone else thought I would be fine, she understood my tears were not just for me. They were for every girl that just wanted to fit in with her friends and family, but were not quite sure of her true identity. This was a lonely place. This was something that people may have thought was ridiculous, but I felt it intensely. This was my sore spot. That girl looking back at me became my ointment. She made me feel like I wasn't alone. She shared my passion, my pain, and purpose.

How often are we isolated by labels, status quos, flaws, or differences? What happens to a person whose identity doesn't fit into one box? I was too Puerto Rican to be Black and too Black to be Puerto Rican. My reflection freed me from trying to figure out exactly which box I fit in to. We all experience life. The circumstances are different, but the emotions are the same. Whatever the flaw, whether it's your hair, ears, eyes, or a leg: it doesn't matter. I know how it feels to want to feel beautiful. I can relate to those tears. My desire today is to be that reflection of hope for other people. It may not be as superficial as a hair-do, but I know pain. I know struggle, ridicule, abuse, low self-esteem, loneliness, and being misunderstood. I can relate to not being sure of how to cope and not knowing if you can find the strength to overcome. Most importantly, I can relate to tears, and I know there is a purpose in the tears.

Today "Dare II Believe" is on a mission to encourage individuals to believe that they can challenge, encourage, and sharpen other individuals by being a reflection of hope. The belief is to become whatever it is that you felt life has not offered to you. If you feel life has dealt you a bad hand, you deal life a better hand. I wanted desperately for my family and friends to embrace my uniqueness. Today, I embrace and encourage them to embrace their own uniqueness. As you sharpen others, you yourself will be sharpened. Be the change. Be the difference. Be the wild card. Be the revolutionary. Be the voice of hope. Dare to believe, even if by occupation you're just a hair stylist. Be the hairstylist that uses their skills to beautify the world, one client at a time.

My childhood tears are what drove my God-given purpose. My life journey that began as a ridiculed wild-haired child, who wanted to feel better about herself, turned into a lifestyle of helping women transform their self-image from the inside out.

Many times we run from the situations and people that will propel us into our destiny. Sometimes the pain is the perfect precursor to an opportunity filled with purpose.

Where does your struggle lie? Is it in a relationship, a handicap, an environment, an addiction, an illness, or a family secret? Whatever it may be, I believe your opportunity dwells within overcoming that challenge. I challenge you today to make a difference. I challenge you to allow your adversary to teach you something. I challenge you to turn your tears into purpose. I have learned that sometimes when you want to get a clue about what God is doing in your life, paying attention to the adversary is key. Are they trying to defeat you? Then you are purposed to win. Are they treating you like you're worthless? Then you have value. Are they counting you out? Then God has counted you in.

Make a commitment today to discover your purpose and pursue your dreams. Don't allow your pain to be in vain. Make a decision to discover the beauty that was produced from that pain. Make a decision that your struggle will not be your shame. The power lies within you. Your destiny is waiting for you. Find the treasure that is produced in pain and struggle by looking within yourself to find your value. Like a diamond in the rough being discovered after extreme temperature and pressure. If you look within, I'm sure you will discover you are a diamond.... I dare you to believe.

Biography:

Zaneta Aycox is an author, inspirational speaker, and poet. In 2010 she founded Build Faith and Dare to Believe (BFDB), an organization that dares individuals to live on purpose. She is the author of BFDB vol. 1: "It's Your Time". Her second book, BFDB vol. 2: "You Hold The Key", will be published in the fall of 2014.

Contact Information:
www.bfdb.me

Chapter 18
Run Wild and Free

By Udoka Omenukor

I know what it's like to feel knocked down.

To have dreams, hopes, and aspirations that continuously, day after day, get brushed off. There was a time when my identity and self-worth rested on goals, people would knock down my dreams and every time it felt like they knocked out a piece of my heart!

This was how I felt for most of my life. Granted, I've only been around for twenty-something years, but I've seen how deep a hole many amazing, ambitious women are in, from teenagers to eighty year olds and beyond. Once you're stuck in the hole, you fall deeper beneath the ground, away from the light every time someone tells you to repress your dreams.

I'm sick of it!

I hope my story offers you a ladder to help you climb out of the holes you may have fallen into, or feel like you were pushed into, and start running wild and free again.

You see, I'm what my friend likes to call a "third culture kid." I have a Nigerian heritage, but I grew up mostly in the US. Imagine going to school and trying to "fit in" to American culture, then going home and struggle to "fit in" to your family's traditional culture. When you're young it's a hard juggling act, and to reconcile this you kind of create your own personal culture, a third culture.

This is a problem.

This is a problem only because when you start creating your own personal culture, it creates a sense of individuality that when you're young and just feel awkward all the time, doesn't thrive in EITHER of the cultures you're engaged in. I found I couldn't fit in in neither the American culture at school nor my Nigerian culture at home. I never felt like I could really be myself anywhere. Because of that I felt alone and depressed. Sometimes being a third culture kid is lonely.

I would watch TV and see interviews with people like Will Smith, Oprah Winfrey, and of course I loved watching interviews with whomever the hot, young celebrity was at that moment. I didn't quite understand what life was like as an artist or a public figure, but I knew I wanted it. It seemed like they received love and adoration from everywhere, no matter how weird they were (Jim Carrey), no matter what weird style they wore (Madonna), and they still got to do cool things! It just wasn't custom in my family to go to theme parks more than once a year, but on the Disney channel, those kids seemed to do cool fun stuff every week. Of course my parents were kind of anti-anything-fun back then (or that's what I felt like) so I'd think to myself *when I grow up, I'm doing ALL THE THINGS!* Imagine that in a cute little kid voice.

My dream was to just live a life where I could be myself, do what I love, and not have to apologize for it. A life where I could be weird like Jim Carrey, funny like Will Smith, and go to theme parks whenever I wanted. I wanted my work to be as fun as what I saw on TV. I knew it was possible because, "I saw it on TV!" This was my little girl logic, but I was on to something. A life where you can just be yourself and do work you love was what my heart desired.

I felt like I had been brain-washed. Coupled with the American motto of, "You can grow up to be anything you want to be!" I felt disillusioned. When I'd turn off the TV or would leave my American school for the day, I'd come home to a message that was more like "You can grow up to be anything you want to be, which is either a pharmacist, doctor, or lawyer."

But I didn't want to be a pharmacist. I was really into all-natural products (yes, at the age of 12). I did not want to be a doctor, it looked like a dull job with no windows and everything was white and grey. I didn't know if I wanted to be a lawyer either. My options felt so limited based upon the options my parents set before me, but when I watched TV the possibilities for other people seemed ENDLESS. Why couldn't my life be as limitless? I felt like a limitless life was not an option for me just because I was born as myself. This really tore me down.

"So how come I can't be a ballerina, actress, zoologist, or another random job I saw on TV that I thought was cool?" I'd ask the adults in my life.

"Well, you're black. You have an accent. You weren't born here. You're female." was the rebuttal. My mom would sometimes add, "You have to be exceptional to succeed in life doing those things, and you can't even keep your room clean."

I internalized this as a personal attack. I thought, *Well, all of those things are true about me.* I thought the only thing holding me back from the dream life I wanted was the mere fact that I was born as me. I really thought that if I had been born as someone else, all these possibilities would be open to me. I began a journey of trying to be someone else. Someone who I thought was successful. Someone, anyone, as long as it wasn't ME. At age thirteen I desperately tried to come up with fun ways to earn money to prove my independence and to prove that, at least in the good ole' US of A, none of those things mattered, but I failed, which made me take all the excuses of why I couldn't live my dream life to heart.

I took this mentality with me through middle school and high school. I passed by opportunities and kept my heart away from what I truly wanted because I believed that I could never have what I truly, truly wanted in my life — Freedom to be myself and love what I do.

I went to college. I tried to study computer science. I'm naturally gifted in math and I was always online. It was a "logical" fit, even though I yearningly gazed at the Arts department building every time I walked by it to get to my math classes on the other side of campus. I kept trying to do what was logical, because by now I believed all the excuses I had been told growing up. But I had a little more freedom in college, so I decided, "Let me give my passions a try," and started a hip-hop dance club. I started auditioning for dance gigs and began building my reputation as a dancer and performance artist. My parents weren't too thrilled about this. In fact, they were practically livid. I'm sure they couldn't stand to see their only daughter head down a path they believed to be a total dead-end.

Throughout my college career there was a constant struggle with my parents and within myself. I felt like I was in a hole, and I could never climb out. I had desires and passions that I couldn't keep suppressed. Every time they arose, they'd get swatted down by someone close to me, pushing me back down into the hole, in the name of trying to help me be realistic. I'd try to talk myself into being "okay" with that. I told myself to focus on my computer science degree, but then it'd happen again and again, until I fell into another bout of depression and was diagnosed with Attention-Deficit Disorder. ADD is a learning disability that is often not taken very seriously. People self-diagnose themselves or their children with ADD because they feel they're easily distracted. As someone with the test results to support it, I –have to say that studying or working in an environment that does not support your dreams and passions when you have ADD is a good way to become a miserable person.

I don't think ADD is as serious as being diagnosed with cancer or anything, but whenever you get a diagnosis, it is usually followed by a big wake up call. My journey started at that point when I realized that all the conventional study and productivity advice I'd been using to bandage my lack of passion for computer science wouldn't work on me because I just think differently. My doctor tried some medications on me, and I just wasn't happy. Making A's in a major I don't like, that I don't even fit in with, that my advisor even told me to consider dropping, is NOT worth mood swings, dehydration, or insomnia.

I asked my doctor "What did people do before medication?" and I kid you not, his response was "They just chose professions they were passionate about. You know. Like photography."

I don't think I could hide my expression. I'm sure my jaw dropped.

From that day forward, I became determined to climb out of the hole.

So of course the resistance I was met with from family, friends, and even within myself became stronger, because I was trying harder than ever to climb out of my hole. The funny thing about fighting for your passions is when you start fighting harder, the world reminds you about the laws of physics. For every action there is an equal and opposite reaction. Your strength for defending your passions will be met by resistance from family, friends, and sometimes even a part of yourself with equal strength. The pushback was strong and hurt a lot emotionally, mentally, and financially. I often felt like I couldn't go on, but I wasn't willing to give up the fight. I was willing to fight to get out of my hole for the rest of my life if I had to.

Cut to now. I haven't given you every juicy detail of my story, but I have to say that I finally — FINALLY feel like I am out of the hole. Exactly how I got out would be a whole other book by itself. I believe what works will be different for everyone, but it takes dedication. Dedication to keeping your passion alive and dedication to your self-improvement. I've tried self-help books, workshops, life coaches, experiential programs (like burlesque dancing, for example, ooh la la), e-courses, dating different guys, therapists, hypnosis, neuro- linguistic programming (NLP), different religions, you name it I've probably tired it. Some things work better than others, but teaching you about what techniques work and which ones don't is out of the scope of my story. I just want to let you know dear reader, that if you keep going, you'll make it. Every action I took toward my passions and my self-development was a part of helping me figure out what I needed to help me get out of my hole. Now, I'm not yet totally clear. Sometimes I may get pushed and trip and stumble back in, but at least now I've got a ladder. I can get out as quickly as I fell in, and I never fall all the way to the bottom. If you get my analogy, probably over doing it now, but at this point, it's a matter of "fall down seven times, stand up eight."

Now I am a HUGE advocate for following your dreams, and it's not easy. It really isn't. Whether you have the most supportive family in the world or you're on your own, boot-strapping it all along the way, it is hard. But as a dream chaser, you don't know how else to live. This is what you're here for.

Maybe you're still stuck in your hole and you're waiting for your "Ok, I Have to get out of here!" rock-bottom moment to give you the kick you need to fight. Maybe you're fighting the good fight right now. Maybe you just recently got out of the hole and are learning how to walk on land again. I want you to know that you're not alone. No matter your gender, heritage, or appearance, you're not alone, and you can do this!

I have so many stories to share, but I want to leave you with this: Do not stop! Even if you have to "compromise" for now, do not stop dreaming and going for your passion and purpose.

Eventually, even if it takes years, the right supportive people will join your side.

Eventually, even if it takes years, the right mentor will guide your path.

Eventually, even if it takes years, you will melt the thoughts that bind you to a life of dissatisfaction.

Eventually, even if it takes years, you will hit GOLD — falling in love with your passion and purpose and actually living it every day.

Eventually, even if it takes years, you will figure out how to get out of your hole and run wild and free.

Biography:

Udoka Omenukor is a twenty something blogger for www.girlaftercollege.net where she writes about her journey to live a life of her own passionate design. She loves interviewing inspirational women, dance of all forms, and the science of nutrition. She's in graduate school studying clinical nutrition and is a competitive aerial artist.

Contact Information:
www.girlaftercollege.net

Chapter 19
Magick Can Happen

By Sheelagh McGrath

I was five years old in 1950 when I left post-war London for Southern Rhodesia – known today as Zimbabwe – in southern Africa. My father, a Royal Air Force Flight Lieutenant, was to be stationed there for a time, as Southern Rhodesia was still under British colonial rule. We left our home in England one cold November morning and took the suburban train into London, at the start of our epic journey. My mother, dressed in a greenish tweed suit and wearing black high heels and a matching handbag with leather gloves, held my hand. My father, carrying his brown leather Gladstone bag, and looking very handsome in his uniform, strode along beside us. I remember feeling very important in my double-breasted, grey worsted coat with its velvet collar and my new patent shoes. Butterflies were fluttering in my stomach, playing some sort of jumping game.

We arrived at Waterloo station, surfacing like moles from the London Underground, onto the platform with the big black steam engines all around. What a lot of clanking and hissing, the huge engines pushing out great puffs of white smoke! A strange smell of smoggy smoke pervaded the air. A muffled voice was broadcasting, "Train leaving platform 8 for Southampton."

With hasty goodbyes to my grandparents and amid much excitement, we boarded the train, looking for our First Class carriage. Commissioned officers in the British military were granted that privilege. The seats were very plush and comfy. The whistle blew, and we were off, amidst cheering relatives and waving friends.

Africa? I wondered what it would be like. With lots of unknown people and wild animals, it was a little scary. I had my first creepy feelings of terror. Suddenly there was our ship. *HMS Stirling Castle*, an enormous vessel. The train ran right alongside it, into the Customs shed; we had arrived at Southampton docks. Through Customs, and out the other side onto the dock, we mounted the gangway up to the deck. I felt like one of the Royal Princesses. All I needed to do was to turn at the top of the gangway and wave, and I would be on the front page of the newspaper. Ah, the stuff of dreams.

What a voyage it would be … I left as a girl in England to begin my life of world travel.

Africa, for a young girl such as myself, was life-changing. The climate, culture, and spirituality were all so different from my home in England. After three years in Africa, my father's tour of duty was completed and we returned to England, leaving Africa and all its mysteries behind.

Fast-forward 20 years …

At 28, I was an established actress in London, married to my wonderful husband, Guy, with one child and another on the way. Africa beckoned and we decided to return to that magickal continent. While raising my two girls, I continued my acting career in TV, radio, and theatre. I won Best Actress for my leading role in the stage production of *St Joan*, one of my proudest moments.

Rhodesia erupted in war in the early 1970s as it moved from colonial rule to independence. After six years of living through the unsettled times of the Rhodesian Bush War, we moved to South Africa, where my third child was born.

Never feeling settled in South Africa, due to the inevitable changes taking place, three years later we took a giant leap of faith and set our faces towards the United States of America.

Our 'Florida adventure' began with great hopes and became 'The Year from Hell!' I thought, at times, that it was our end.

We joined a fellow Rhodesian in an entrepreneurial adventure in Florida. Shocks were waiting. Our start up business never really thrived. My husband was depressed. He felt he was a failure; we had three children and no funds. I knew, somehow, that everything would be okay. I was working three jobs to keep us going. That year was a very big strain upon all of us; however, I managed to hold it all together.

As fate would have it, my husband's previous boss in South Africa was now running the same company in America. Fulfilling a premonition I experienced in South Africa, he came to our rescue; recruiting my husband for a position in New England.

Magick happened!

It was a long, arduous drive up to Boston but full of hope and gratitude. We were on the road again to another new adventure! Guided once again by my Spiritual connection, which had been with me all my life.

But … such adventures take their toll.

We settled into our next new life, and my children went through all the teething troubles of a new country. New culture, new school, new friends… New England – but not my England.

We had come to live in a harbor town, south of Boston, in the beautiful summertime. I had put away money from the sale of our home in South Africa, which we could now use as a deposit on a house. Hallelujah!

Summertime gave way to fall, then winter. The weather got very cold. We had no extended family and no firm friends as yet. The locals seemed to fade away into their homes, and the warm summer friendliness had crawled away into icy hibernation.

That first Christmas in New England was sad and lonely, as I realized how isolated we were as a family. People around us were talking about family Thanksgiving and Christmas gatherings with their familiar traditions.

Where were ours? We had left them behind in England, Rhodesia, and South Africa – our choice. We hadn't thought about the repercussions. Life was always going to be exciting and adventurous, although, in the depths of my soul, I longed to return to the "Country of my Birth."

Christmas came and went, and it was cold beyond belief. There were walks where I would come back stimulated by the cold, then the contrast of a heated home would hit, followed by extreme tiredness and sleepiness. Temperatures had fallen way below freezing!

By February, my spirits were beginning to sag. We couldn't afford to escape to "ski country" or book a sunny holiday. The short days and early darkness began to depress me. Things seemed so unfamiliar. I was sinking slowly into a dark, hopeless pit. I had no one to talk to and began to feel like a prisoner in my own life. Where was the friendliness and sunshine of southern Africa?

The phone rang, oh Glory Be, it was Jean, my darling friend from South Africa! "How are you Sheels?" "Not good", I replied. I had never said that before.

"I want you to immerse yourself in a bath of warm water with bath salts and lay back with your head in the water, as far as you can while still being able to breathe."

This was the advice my dearest friend in the world gave me, from across the ocean, in another hemisphere. Without question, I took her advice, so glad that someone who really knew me was caring for me. I stayed enveloped in that warm cocoon with such a sense of relief and calm, knowing that my friend wouldn't let me drown in this morass of unpleasant feelings.

Out of the bath, and the phone rang again. Jean's warm voice said, "I have booked you a ticket to Johannesburg. Ask Guy if the dates are okay, and call me back." No money and I was going back to Africa. What a friend! Oh joy!

Although I had some trepidation about leaving my girls, I was not much good to anyone in this state. My husband agreed and said he'd manage the girls and the home 'til I returned in six weeks. Immediately, I felt lighter, and soon I was winging my way back to the magickal spirit of southern Africa.

After six weeks of healing and laughter and regaining my old self, seeing my parents in the Cape, and visiting with friends and family, I was ready to return to the States and my little family.

Refreshed, I knew I could take on anything, or so I thought.

That summer my sister and her husband came to visit. It was a difficult visit – such negativity! Then came my mother-in-law, who was grieving the recent deaths of her daughter and husband. Their turmoil and grief proved all too much for me. The emotional crash I had been avoiding, happened then. Our Florida experience, the cold dark New England winter, and continued upheaval brought me to breaking point.

So how had my life come to this?

This once excited little girl who had journeyed to Africa full of hopes and dreams now suddenly found herself in a desperate state of mind, aged 38 in yet another strange land.

I fell into a downward spiral.

I lay in my bed, not wanting to get up or go out.

I had constant headaches and fatigue.

The fears and anxiety were horrific.

Losing weight, I would forget to eat.

The worst of it was the persistent insomnia. As I reached the edge of sleep, I would come to, in a panic with the fear that if I fell asleep I would either go mad or die.

I lost my sense of self! I didn't know ME anymore; who was I?

I was frightened of the unknown,

My poor children without a mother, and there was nothing I could do!

My husband should have found me professional help, but I think he was frightened too. Frightened that if he let me go, I'd never come back.

Things were reaching fever pitch.

I prayed at night for the healing my spirit so badly needed. The words, "It's an aberration of the mind," kept running through my head!

I can only describe my spiritual journey at this time as walking on the floors of Hell.

I prayed and prayed with no outside help or friends.

I atoned for all the wrongs I had ever caused.

My relationships with my husband and children were thoroughly examined, my shortcomings laid bare.

I asked forgiveness from Above for any pain I had ever caused, and I was never so vulnerable in my life, or so wretched.

It was the Dark Night of the Soul.

Then God and my Angels gently steered me back to my Spiritual Source.

Just like the Phoenix rising from the Ashes, with my Spiritual connection restored, I found new life. With the support of my family, a wonderful family counselor, and acquaintances from before my downfall, now friends, I began to stand on my own feet again.

Eventually, I attended the University of Massachusetts to study psychology. The healing had begun. I was beginning to retrieve my confidence.

I have experienced other very frightening moments in my life, among them a dreadful car accident from which I barely escaped with my life, but that's for another time.

Suffice it to say, through the years I have come to know myself, my source of spirit, and discovered a strength, which I never knew I possessed until those times of trial.

Angels watch over us and, when we call upon them, they do help. Like "Magick," our nightmares turn into beautiful dreams.

Magick doesn't always happen instantly but when we send our good intentions into the Universe, I believe, our Spiritual Guides and Angels aid in manifesting our wishes in "Divine Timing." My legacy will be that I have helped many people, in many ways, in many places with healing words of wisdom, channeled from the Divine Spirit of God.

Happiness is being in tune with our soul and being guided by that beautiful energy that belongs to us all: Oneness ... Forgiveness ... Acceptance ... Empowerment for self and others ... Enlightenment! Believe in your self-worth and, in unison with your Spiritual Hotline, YOU can make MAGICK happen!

Biography:

Sheelagh McGrath was born in London, amidst the Blitz of WWII. She studied drama, psychology and healing modalities. She has excelled in a variety of talented pursuits, including as a professional actress, teacher, Natural Therapies practitioner, writer, wife, mother and grandmother, spending her adult life in the UK, southern Africa, USA, and Australia where she continues to pursue her mission: "to empower others to empower themselves."

Contact Information:
sheelagh@sheelaghmcgrath.com
swannop@bigpond.net.au

Chapter 20
The Light at the End of the Tunnel

By Win Charles

When I was born on June 22, 1987, I weighed only one pound, thirteen ounces. I still hold the record for being the smallest baby ever born at Aspen Valley Hospital in Aspen, Colorado. Because of my small weight and the many risks associated with a premature birth I was immediately flown to Denver, 200 miles away, to the third best children's hospital in the nation. After many tests, I was diagnosed with cerebral palsy.

"Put her in an institution!" one doctor insisted.

My parents said, "No way!"

Then my dad told the doctor, "Let's move on. What's next?"

"Cerebral palsy is a group of disorders that can involve brain and nervous system functions, such as movement, hearing, seeing, speaking, learning, and thinking." (Wikipedia.org).

CP is like having a constant trauma happening to your brain, like your brain is being banged on over and over. One result is that you simply can't sit up straight, because you have little or no core body strength. That brain trauma can cause huge difficulties in walking and speaking, as well as a spine condition called scoliosis, where the spine is curved away from its normal alignment. Nine out of ten people who have CP also have scoliosis. As a person with CP grows older, usually by the teen years, that person will likely need surgery to correct the scoliosis, because the spine is compressing the internal organs, such as lungs, stomach, and heart.

By age six, I could clearly see that my friends were fully functioning. There's a photo of my first grade class at Aspen Country Day School. I'm in the photo of course, but it's obvious that I'm somewhat different from my classmates, as I sit off center, leaning away from the other kids. It certainly wasn't because I didn't like them! I simply couldn't hold myself up in the chair.

When I was in seventh grade, my mom was driving me to school one day when she stopped the car. She told me, "You have a disability."

She said it was called cerebral palsy, and she gave me the call letters CP. "Cerebral" meant the damage was in the brain, and "palsy" meant that parts of the brain were constantly struggling to shake off the trauma of not having enough oxygen coming through the blood vessels. While I was being born so very early and so very small, the CP almost killed me.

From the day that Mom first told me about CP, until the day she died when I was twenty-three years old, my feisty and courageous mother never stopped telling me that I could do anything and overcome everything.

A few years later, I was asked to make a presentation to my high school English class about my condition. After I researched CP and learned more about what I was facing, I closed my laptop and cried.

But my tears did not last long. Mom was my rock. She was constantly encouraging me to be independent and to work things out for myself. If people ridiculed me or discounted me she would say, "You know why they do that, don't you? They're afraid of the unknown. Fear is *their* disability."

So I learned that if you keep moving forward, the dark shadows are no more than passing scenery.

Unlike many people who don't know what they want to do, I knew by tenth grade that I wanted an education degree.

There have been three pivotal moments in my life when I could have said that the light at the end of a tunnel was the headlight of an oncoming train. What I learned though, is that you can always find something good in life. I look for roses as my "something good," because I love them. I named my digital art business after them: Aspen Rose Arts. Every important moment in my life has taught me that *there are always some roses*, even in a dark tunnel.

The first pivotal moment happened when I was eighteen, shortly before my nineteenth birthday, and was having surgery on my back to correct the scoliosis. Before the surgery, people were telling me, "You need to write your story." Even though I had CP, I was a typical teenager, living in the fast lane, without a care in the world. I could walk unaided.

The moment is etched in my memory. On June 16, 2006, I was coming out of anesthesia and mumbling, "Why am I here?" For some reason I was much weaker than I ever expected to be. I had no core body strength and was groggy from pain medication. Two people, a physical therapist and a nurse, had to literally support me as I sat up on the edge of the bed.

Mom was in the room, too. She looked at me and said, "You can do this."

It turned out that I was allergic to the anesthetic they used. During surgery, my spine went "dead" for about 20 minutes. The surgery failed. After it I could no longer walk unaided. My mom was encouraging me even before I knew what had happened to my walking ability.

Mom stayed with me for three days while I was in the ICU in critical condition. *How critical?* Well, they had to resuscitate me eleven times. I spent my nineteenth birthday in the hospital.

The second pivotal moment began in July 2010. While I was a volunteer at a kids' art camp, and Mom was supposed to join me there for the weekend, she went instead to Aspen Valley Hospital (AVH) because she had an unusually painful headache. They gave her two bags of IV fluids and sent her home.

At the time, my mom's sister was visiting from The Bahamas. When Mom came home from AVH with the IV bags, my aunt noticed within minutes that something worse than a headache was going on. Mom seemed to be in a daze; her eyes were crossed and her speech was slurred. Back to AVH she went, where the staff immediately airlifted her to Denver on a helicopter life flight.

In the Denver hospital they put my mom into a medically-induced coma. I got there shortly after that. One afternoon around four o'clock, as I came into her room, all the medical machines went off at the same time, beeps and whistles going a mile a minute. Mom was in a coma with a a trachea tube in her throat. I was scared of all the machine noises, and scared to see my mom, my rock, lying so helpless in the hospital bed.

A ventilator was breathing for her. A heart monitor was beeping out her heart rate. Even though it was smaller than the ventilator, the heart monitor made a louder sound. There was a third monitor near the bed, too, one that measured the level of oxygen in Mom's blood. It too made a sound.

Her eyes were closed, but I said, "I love you, Mom," and I kept saying it over and over. Maybe I said it a hundred times.

Some medical people say that people in a coma can't hear, but I *know* that my mom heard me.

We communicated telepathically, as I asked her – right there in that hospital room while she was in a coma – about writing my memoir. *Should I do it?*

She simply told me, "Yes."

My heaven-sent mom passed away from a brain aneurysm on August 12, 2010.

That was almost four years ago, and I can tell you that watching Mom die was worse than my own back surgery pain and the loss of my ability to walk normally.

The most important thing I learned is that you cannot take life for granted and you can't take any of your abilities or talents for granted either, "Use them or lose them". We have to pay attention to the important moments, because they're telling us that this physical life is too short, over before we know it.

Make the most of *everything* while you're here. *Stop and smell those roses!*

My memoir *I, Win* was published in October 2012.

My third pivotal moment began just recently, when I asked a staff member at AVH for my medical records to be transferred to the hospital in Denver, where I will soon be having surgery to correct a deviated septum.

Now a deviated septum is not caused by CP. Even people without CP can fall down. But because I have CP and no one was close enough to catch me as I fell, I landed on my nose, and it ended up broken.

The septum is the divider between the two nasal cavities, and "deviated" means the septum got out of alignment. It went crooked. I have sounded very nasal ever since I fell on my nose.

A deviated septum can shut down the nasal cavities, and *that* can cause sleep apnea, which means you stop breathing while you're sleeping.

Back in 2006, during the surgery to correct the scoliosis, we learned that I'm allergic to a certain drug that's used as an anesthetic. It's called Propofol, and the bad reaction to it is called Propofol Infusion Syndrome.

So to make sure that the hospital staff would not use Propofol during surgery to correct the deviated septum, I asked the AVH people to transfer my medical files – with the notation about my allergy to Propofol – to the Denver hospital where I'd be having the nose job.

To my horror, the person said, "It's not in the records."

Naturally I asked "*Why not?*"

"They forgot to document it."

That was a huge reminder to keep two steps ahead of everyone, and always pay attention to details. My way of being vigilant is to ask questions, lots and lots of them. After all, it's my life. Deviated septum or not, I want to smell as many roses as I can, even if they are in a dark tunnel!

In 2012, things turned around for me in a huge way when I published my memoir *I, Win.* And in case you haven't guessed yet, it *is* dedicated to my family, especially my mom.

Since the book was published, I've been teaching non-disabled people how to get over their fear of the disabled. Physically, mentally, and psychologically, I help people disconnect from an upbringing that says disabled people are "other than" or "less than" normal.

One person who read this chapter before it went into print wanted me to use certain words and phrases here, besides "other than" and "less than" to describe the disabled. But I cannot do it. Those words are so hurtful – and every disabled person has already heard them too many times – that I could break down crying just by mentioning them. You know the words I mean, the words I don't want to use even here. Repeating them would just add them to the collective unconscious again. Certain words are simply unacceptable, it's best that everyone just forget them.

Instead, I will use words like "beautiful" and "self-confident" to describe myself. I have faced many challenges in my life, and I hope that the way I'm facing them will inspire other people to deal with their own challenges. I accept that I am a beautiful woman with a message to share with the world.

If people don't want to support me or don't want to hear what I have to say, that's fine. I am not looking to add points to my Permanent Record in heaven. I want to be a positive role model for people who have difficulty speaking up for themselves, people who get discouraged and think it's time to quit trying, people who can't seem to make their dreams come true. I want to inspire people with my message: "Anything is possible."

In 2013, I competed in the Kona Ironman Triathlon, the most grueling sports competition in the world (the "tri" refers to swimming, bicycling, and running). I was the first woman with CP to ever compete at Kona, which has been an international competition for about thirty years. Most professional triathletes spend a year or more training for Kona. I started training in March of that year, going to the gym three times a week for an hour each time. I also trained on the Alter-G machine, a recumbent bike, and a recumbent spin bike.

Doing what I do now... you could call it a mission: I'm writing books and speaking out in public about accepting people for *who they are.* Every individual, whether disabled or not, is a valuable human being whose life adds to our own, as our lives add to theirs. What goes around, comes around.

Whatever your challenge, and we all have them, I know that you will find your own light at the end of *your* tunnel.

Biography:

Win Charles is an athlete, an author, and an artist. She is here to empower people. She can help you realize that you *can* achieve your dreams, no matter what challenges you face, even if they seem insurmountable, even if they would be hard for anyone to endure. She is here to inspire you to take your dream to the next level, as she has done.

Contact Information:
www.authorwincharles.com

Sneak Peak

I AM Tunda

By Tunda Wannamaker

I remember the first time the teacher called my name in kindergarten and my classroom bursting into laughter because she was having a hard time pronouncing it. She was a little frustrated and said, "How the heck do I say this?"

I knew she was talking about me from the stuttering of the T's, so I said with a soft voice, "Tunda." She replied, "Well that's different." It didn't bother me that she called me different, in fact, it made me feel special that she could see it, because even at a young age, there was something that I already knew, that there was something different about me.

Of course the kids thought otherwise. I was ridiculed at lunch, on the playground, in the hallway, or wherever there wasn't a teacher present. As I grew older, so did my classmates, and the jokes became more hurtful. I learned to listen to them, not the hurtful words directed to me, but I began to listen to the hurt coming from them. The saying "hurt people, hurt people" is really true at any age. After a while and some grades later, it continued. I found myself numb to the taunting and began to really listen to the voice from within. Every time I would hear something that was not in alignment to who I was, I would hear a small voice from within saying, *It will be okay. You are different, you were not created to fit in, but you were created to make a difference….*

To read the rest of the story, stay tuned to the next *20 Beautiful Women* to be released in 2015.

Biography:

Tunda Wannamaker is a spiritual life coach, motivator, alignment specialist, and truth seeker. She has worked on some of the most successful events in the industry, including Tyler Perry plays, Kirk Franklin, Yolanda Adams, E Lynn Harris, and many more. She has a love for pushing others to their highest potential. She awakens the discernment in others so that they may pursue their life purpose. She teaches you how to take any negative situation and turn it into something positive. Tunda believes we all have the ability to create the thing that is lacking in our life. She teaches you to face your fears and to overcome personal challenges to create the life you are destined to have.

Contact Information:
www.facebook.com/tundawannamaker
www.twitter.com/tundawannamaker
www.coverediam.com

We were all created to do something, and the answer is on the inside, awaiting the awakening.

Are You Beautiful?

Share With Us Your Story!
Email story@20beautifulwomen.com for the opportunity to be in the next book.

Did you love the book?

Tell the world:
#20beautifulwomen on all your social media sites and share why you loved it!

Made in the USA
San Bernardino, CA
23 August 2014